AF572259

FAILURE FREEDOM

PAUL DE JONG

ENDORSEMENTS

Pastor Paul has brought a truth that is life-changing. If we can get our minds around the message in Failure Freedom and really practice it in our lives, things will change. It's freeing and encouraging. Paul de Jong clearly shows how we learn and grow in our failures, not when everything seems good and easy. God has called you to a good life, not an easy one. So, fail your way forward and fail your way to success. You will be so glad you read Failure Freedom.

Casey Treat
Senior Pastor, Christian Faith Center, Seattle, USA

Pastor Paul de Jong's new book is insightful and encouraging We can all learn from his powerful revelations on the freedom to fail: how failure is a part of every person's life and how we can use it as fuel for our future and a greater walk with the Lord.

Jentezen Franklin
Senior Pastor, Free Chapel, Author of The New York Times' Best Seller, Fasting

Pastor Paul de Jong's message on failure will make a real difference in every person's life. Paul gets to the bottom line issues that keep many from success. Read this and apply it and you will grow in your faith and be encouraged and inspired to move forward and walk out your God-given dreams.

Tommy Barnett
Pastor, Phoenix First, Founder, LA & Phoenix Dream Centers

Having known Paul for many, many years his honesty, transparency and real approach to life and ministry has blessed my life immensely. This book will help you discover your real self and help you reach your God potential.

Ps Danny Guglielmucci
Founding Leader, Edge Church International

Anyone who wants to grow a great life has to learn how to fail well. Failure is not optional. It will happen and many times our failing is actually what leads to our succeeding. Paul tackles such an important issue in this book, as too many have let failure define them instead of refine them. This book will encourage you to get back up and try again, it will cheer you on from the place failure tells you to stop and it will give you faith to face the fear.

Charlotte Gambill
Lead Pastor, Life Church

In Failure Freedom, Paul de Jong explores the wild territory we must all navigate in order to fulfill our God-given potential: our mistakes. With compelling insight, biblical truth, and personal wisdom based on experience, Paul provides a roadmap for moving through failure and coming out stronger, smarter, and sharper on the other side. If you want to be liberated from the liabilities of your past, then Failure Freedom is a must-read.

Chris Hodges
Senior Pastor, Church of the Highlands, Author of Fresh Air and Four Cups

I have failed before and I will fail again. My responses would have been much more mature had I read Failure Freedom by my friend Paul de Jong. But it's not too late to learn and grow. I still will need Pastor Paul de Jong's wisdom as long as I live. This is a most freeing book you will read.

Dr. Sam Chand
Leadership Consultant and author of
Cracking Your Church's Culture Code
(www.samchand.com)

Everyone wants to succeed. Nobody likes to fail. Most of us are intimidated and diminished by worries about messing up. Yet, in his book, Failure Freedom, Pastor Paul de Jong illuminates this unfounded fear and exposes it for the insignificant hindrance it truly is. The fear of failure can paralyze and even enslave us from the liberty and victory that God desires, but that doesn't have to be. If you've ever struggled with this fear, Paul's remarkably honest book will shed light on the truth that failure is just an opportunity to come one step closer to freedom in God. Failure is just another way to finally be free!

Steve Kelly
Senior Pastor, Wave Church

I have known Paul de Jong for nearly his whole life and can testify of his character, loyalty and pastoral heart towards people. I have no doubt that his own journey of faith and freedom from failure will encourage and strengthen your walk with Christ, and give you practical tools to overcome that which has been holding you back.

Brian Houston
Senior Pastor, Hillsong Church

PUBLISHED BY:

Paul de Jong Ministries
95 Mt Eden Road, Mt Eden
Auckland 1023
New Zealand

PO Box 108138
Symonds Street, Auckland 1150
New Zealand

P: +64 9 306 4222
F: +64 9 306 4223
Email: paul.dejong@lifenz.org

Copyright @ Paul de Jong, 2015

The right of Paul de Jong to be identified as the author of this work in terms of section 96 of the Copyright Act 1994 is hereby asserted.

TEXT DESIGNED BY:

Jessica Holdaway

Printed in New Zealand by McCollams Print

ISBN 978-0-473-30409-6
A catalogue record for this book is available from the National Library of New Zealand

All rights reserved. No part of this book may be reprinted or reproduced or utilised in any form or by any electronic, mechanical or other means, now known or hereafter invented, including photocopying and recording or in any information storage or retrieval system, without permission in writing from the publisher.

COVER DESIGNED BY:

Jessica Holdaway

CONTENTS

FOREWORD

Paul de Jong is one of the most practical Bible teachers I know. He has the uncanny ability to take biblical truths and make them relevant to our daily lives. In fact, I relate to his teachings so much that whenever I read his books, I find myself thinking, That's me! That's me! And Failure Freedom is no different. In it, Paul shows us how we can learn from our mistakes and find freedom in our failures.

We were all born in bondage as slaves to sin, but there is a yearning in all of us to be free. I am always amazed when people talk about being free and don't realize they're actually still in bondage. Jesus talks about this type of bondage in John 8:31–33: *"Then Jesus said to those Jews who believed Him, 'If you abide in My word, you are My disciples indeed. And you shall know the truth, and the truth shall make you free.' They answered Him, 'We are Abraham's descendants, and have never been in bondage to anyone. How can You say, "You will be made free"?'"* It might seem unusual, but verse 33 is one of my favorite verses in the Bible! As you read it again, think about what these Jews are saying: "We are Abraham's descendants and have never been in bondage to anyone." The irony is they had been in bondage to everyone! And when they made this statement, they were in bondage to the Romans. They were slaves right then, yet they said, "We've never been in bondage to anyone."

This scripture proves that bound people don't know they're bound. If a person does not know the Lord, he's in bondage, but he doesn't know he's in bondage. It's just like the old saying, "Deceived people don't know they're deceived." Yet in John 8, Jesus was talking to the Jews who believed in Him. So is it possible for believers to be bound or deceived and not know it? Absolutely! We can be in bondage to lines of thought or past failures. We can also be in bondage to things that control us such as overeating, drugs, alcohol, nicotine, lust, pornography, anger, bitterness, unforgiveness, resentment, hate, malice, envy, jealousy, insecurity, inferiority, rejection, fear … the list goes on. In verses 34–36, Jesus makes it clear who's in bondage: *"Jesus answered them, 'Most assuredly, I say to you, whoever commits sin is a slave of sin. And a slave does not abide in the house forever, but a son abides forever. Therefore if the Son makes you free, you shall be free indeed.'"*

God is in the business of rescuing people. If you're reading this book and you're in bondage, don't feel bad. Don't feel guilty. You're not alone— I think we can all say we need a measure of rescuing from our mistakes. You've come to the right place.

This book will help you find freedom from the bondage of past failures and learn from those failures so you can turn them into success. Paul has spoken at Gateway Church on several occasions and is one of the most well-received speakers we've had, and I believe one of the reasons is because of his humility and transparency about his own struggles. He's a man who's persevered to allow God to teach him through trials, and now we have the opportunity to learn from his revelation of finding true freedom in failure.

I encourage you to pray that God would open your heart and mind as you read this book and that He would lead you to a new knowledge of what it truly means to be free.

Robert Morris

Founding Senior Pastor, Gateway Church, Dallas/Fort Worth, Texas

Bestselling Author of The Blessed Life, From Dream to Destiny, The God I Never Knew, and The Blessed Church

ABOUT THE AUTHOR

Paul and his wife Maree are the pioneers and Senior Leaders of LIFE, a church that focuses on four areas: Church, Community, Business and Kingdom (www.lifenz.org). LIFE began in 1991 in Auckland, New Zealand, and today is a multi-campus, multinational church, which continues to beat with the original dream of seeing its city changed, its nation influenced and the world touched.

Under Paul and Maree's leadership, LIFE has grown throughout its many campuses, and continues to impact multiple thousands of people, pastors and leaders through a number of conferences that are held annually. Along with the many Kingdom initiatives, LIFE owns and has developed an increasing number of businesses, which fund an ever-expanding community arm.

Paul travels extensively, speaking at leadership conferences, churches and business environments across the globe. He is also the inspiration for a wide range of leadership development initiatives including a website, www.pauldejongnz.com, that continue to inspire and equip people from all streams of life. Paul's passion and mission is 'to live and lead by example'. He believes we discover our full potential only when we live an authentic, faith-inspired, God-dependent life.

ACKNOWLEDGMENTS

Firstly, I want to thank Jesus, for the way He has been with me and led me every day of my life. It is His grace, faithfulness, love and wisdom which have provided the oxygen to keep me leading and creating, and also being the husband, father and grandfather for my most incredible family.

To my wife, Maree, you are and have always been my best friend and greatest supporter. Your love, inspiration and wisdom have enabled me to grow to where I am today. I love you with all my heart.

To Rachel and Caroline, your help and input while I have been writing this book have been extremely valuable and very much appreciated. Also, thank you to all those who, over many years, have continued to believe in me during my failures, have helped me come to the revelations that are contained in this book and have liberated me to reach higher into all that God has.

Finally, thank you to the members of our amazing LIFE family, who make up the community of people with whom we 'do life'. Your continued love and support have encouraged me to keep reaching beyond what I had believed to be my boundaries; there, I have discovered there is so much more for each person who continues to take a step of faith.

INTRODUCTION

This book is the result of one of my life's most amazing and freeing revelations. The truth is that I've never read it in a book, heard a message on it or even had someone tell me most of what you are about to read. I have discovered that we can all learn how to move out from under the bondage and stronghold of our ongoing failure reality. So much so, that failure, when understood and channelled correctly, can end up becoming one of our greatest assets and, therefore, one of our best friends!

You may be saying: Are you serious, Paul? Can I really reach a place in my life where I don't have to live hiding my mistakes, or cringe in embarrassment about what I have failed to achieve? Surely you don't mean that I could ever actually get to a place where my failures could become my greatest life lessons?

That is exactly what I am saying. There is a place of incredible freedom. It is a place where: our mistakes can become unbelievable assets; we don't have to live a lie or pretend we are close to perfection; and we can look both the past and the present square in the eye and know that failure, whether our own or that of someone else which has caused us pain, has become a learning point for our future. We no longer need to live with the ongoing domination of regret.

There is a place of incredible freedom – a place where our mistakes can become unbelievable assets

---

It may seem impossible to believe right now, but no matter what you have been through, there is a place we can all discover... a place I like to call failure freedom.

I have no doubt that you, like me, are aware that we are confronted by the voice of failure on a consistent basis. What I have come to discover is that if we are to keep living a potential-releasing life, the reality is that we will all continue to fail. This book is about creating an understanding that we don't have to be dominated by the failures of the past, or have the constant pressure of feeling like we are falling short of what we wish we could achieve. It is about learning how we can truly live today in a place of *failure freedom.*

As I share with you about moving from failure regret to failure freedom, I believe that what I have had to personally learn the hard way, will help you create a life of increasing freedom around your own failures. I believe that you too will be able to see failure as a pathway forward to even greater influence, success and significance. Also, that you would come to realise, as I have, that when processed correctly, failure can become a life-long friend, rather than an enemy called limitation.

For me, the idea of you or I being held back from the fullness of life that God has promised because of an incorrect view of failure, is a totally unacceptable thought. I long for all of us to wake up every day with a real sense that nothing – no wrong understanding, no former sin, no insecurity, no false belief, no residual hurt or disappointment – will be able to prevent us from living in the fullness of God's potential.

In [this] freedom Christ has made us free [and completely liberated us]; stand fast then, and do not be hampered and held ensnared and submit again to a yoke of slavery [which you have once put off].
Galatians 5:1 AMP

Living completely under the law only produces an endless stream of boxes requiring our yes or no responses…rights or wrongs…successes or failures. The message and life of Jesus is that a relationship with Him is our answer to freedom. No matter what has gone before or will take place tomorrow, we can live under His word and His grace, and so discover a doorway to failure freedom.

We can all discover a doorway to failure freedom

As you read on, I want to take you on a journey to believing that you too can come to the place where you are living beyond the failure cringe factor, beyond the cover-ups, beyond the defensiveness and beyond the living of a lie. It is possible!

Can I encourage you to keep a notebook or journal beside you as you read? All kinds of memories are going to flood your mind. Write them down. Own them. Accept them as facts of your life – past and present. By the time you get to the final page of this book, my prayer and hope for you is that you see with the eyes of your spirit, these letters scrawled across every page…

F-A-I-L-U-R-E F-R-E-E-D-O-M

FAILURE FREEZE

PART ONE

FROZEN BY FAILURE

CHAPTER ONE

My great concern is not whether you have failed, but whether you are content with failure.
Abraham Lincoln

Have you ever found yourself in a situation where you have failed miserably at something? Can you recall the pain, the sense of disappointment and, at times, even the lasting shame? How did you react?

For me, there were many times where the emotions surrounding failure were so strong that I just tried to suppress and forget about the situation. I often felt unable to move on and, therefore, decided never to try what I had failed in again.

When I was a young man, I grew up being frozen so often by failure. I cannot recall having anyone explain to me that failure is in everyone's world; all I knew to do was to hide and, consequently, I found myself wanting to give up once I did fail. So I know what it's like to be trapped in the cycle of condemnation and shame that comes with failing.

I remember vividly at the age of 19 having my first opportunity to speak at a church that was different to the one in which I had grown up. The pressure I felt in the weeks building up to what I saw as one of the biggest challenges of my life up to that point was immense. Flooded with thoughts of inability and insecurity, under what was extreme pressure, which seemed to magnify as the day drew closer, I put together a message that I believed was right. In fact, I wrote the message out word for word and timed myself over and over, as I had been asked to speak for 40 minutes. The church was a fairly conservative one, with about 50 people in the congregation, who were mostly people of senior years. The morning arrived and I recall that I was so nervous that I had not been able to sleep for more than one hour. We had to drive almost two hours from the Bible College where I was studying. There were a few others with me as well, who were going to lead worship. The internal pressure felt like a water balloon that was about to burst. I so wanted to do it right and not fail God. After the worship, the moment had come for me to speak. The next thing I can remember is finishing my message. I looked at my watch and, to my horror, it had taken all of 10 minutes! I was stunned. I didn't know what to say or do. My face turned a scarlet colour and huge beads of sweat started to roll down my forehead. In a panic, I didn't even pray; I just said 'thank you' and walked off the stage, surrounded in a blanket of despair and despondency. I wanted to run, scream, hide and, definitely, never speak again. Nonetheless, because I was with the team, I had to stay for the rest of the service. My college leader even made me shake the hands of those leaving at the end. I will never forget one elderly lady taking my hand and whispering in my ear, "Great message, sonny". I immediately responded internally with, "That's not true"; I thought maybe she was hard of hearing.

Under the pressure of the moment, doing something I had never done before, I panicked. I read my message so quickly that what should have taken 40 minutes, took 10. It must have been shocking. I was so thankful they didn't record the message!

I am sure you, too, have memories of trying something beyond what you have ever done before and feeling like a failure: feeling as though you never want to get up again, being frozen and not being prepared to try again, ever. Effectively, I was frozen by failure in that area for quite some time until I came to understand I was not alone.

What does being frozen by failure mean? Well, as soon as we place something in a freezer, it instantly begins the process of trapping the item in its original state. The enemy's plan is for our failure to become frozen in time and to remain in its original state, just like that item frozen in a freezer. He wants us to believe it must remain hidden away and never dealt with, and that is often exactly what we feel like doing. We want to run away from our failure, pretend it never happened and move on. However, when we do this, nothing changes and nothing is dealt with or removed. That part of our life is, currently, in what I call a frozen state. Whether the failure has come as a result of our actions or someone's actions towards us, the enemy seeks to hold us in that state where we freeze at failure, rather than process it past the point of pain, to a platform of learning.

Failure freeze is the enemy's plan to reduce our future

WHERE HAS FAILURE FROZEN YOU?

One of the joys of my life is interacting with children. I just love to watch how they go about their learning. Usually, at around the age of one, each child begins to attempt to walk. Having mastered the art of rolling, crawling and finally standing, the desire to walk seems to fully capture their attention. The challenge of letting go of the security of what they are holding onto, versus the desire to do something they were born to do, creates an enormous tension. While standing on their cute, chubby legs, legs that have never ventured into this unknown territory, and with much encouragement from all those around, they finally let go and take their first steps. After one step and then perhaps another, they take what we would all call an expected fall.

Take a moment to think about it from the child's perspective because, the reality is, you were once that child. It is amazing how everybody around that child celebrates the moment of triumph, even though it is actually mixed with much failure. The child falls, as expected, but then they try again, and fail again, while everyone continues to celebrate. We call the relatives; we bring out the cameras; we blow up the balloons. Amongst all this celebrating, the baby gets up again and again and continues the learning process: more steps, more falls. We keep encouraging, they keep getting up and, eventually, they are walking. You see, the greatest of their advancements is based on the learning that results from their failure, and that is true for every part of life!

Unlimited advancement is the result of learning from failure

Unfortunately, as we grow older, the cheering seems to stop and the understanding that failure is always in the equation of success goes unvoiced. Then the day arrives when we fail and we find ourselves alone, with very little encouragement to make another attempt. The pressure of the failure takes centre stage and, instead of getting up and trying again, as we did when we were a small child, we freeze. The shame of making a mistake, of not doing enough or being enough cripples us to the point that we are unable to step out and try again.

I am not sure at what age it happens but, without even knowing it, there is a sudden and deathly silence when we fail. And, instead of being cheered on to try again, we feel like everyone has left the room. This deafening silence can become so loud that it pierces our internal world with a repeating accusation: "You just failed, you just failed, you just failed... you're a failure, you're a failure". As we struggle back to our feet (although, sadly, some of us never do) and look around, we find the cheering crowd has now gone and the inner sense of emptiness dominates so strongly. All of a sudden, we become acutely aware that failure has taken place. No one ever told us that potential continues only when we understand that learning results from the process of falling and rising.

One of the first questions we all need to answer is, "When did I stop getting up?" How old were you when you stopped understanding that you are still human and failure is a crucial part of your development and, also, that failure is in the future of anyone prepared to reach for their God-given potential?

Let's replay the baby's first steps: one step, two steps and then a fall that ends in a bruise or two. Now, imagine if the baby made a decision to never get up again. The extended family leaves, the cameras stop rolling and the party finishes. You see, the baby has failed and there will never be another attempt. I think you can see where I am coming from. We can't give up just because we have experienced failure. We can't freeze and never try again. We must bounce back. We can all learn from our mistakes and can move on into something even greater.

Thank God that He put a stronger drive within the core of us, as children, to keep trying again and again: a drive that is more powerful than is the disappointment we experienced.

Often, we stop getting up because the initial shouts of encouragement have dissipated and have now been replaced by the even louder internal noise of disappointed silence: a feeling of personal embarrassment, or an attitude of "I just simply don't know anymore". Our challenge as adults is that we can allow our minds to accept these defeating thoughts, rather than to see our failure as a God-designed platform of learning.

Failing while trying to succeed is a God-designed platform of learning

---

We all struggle with coming to terms with our own failures. All too often, I have experienced that feeling of hopelessness. Even now, after so many years of understanding the value of failure, I can find myself needing to stop and think, "How much has failure worked its way into me? Am I moving forward or am I frozen by failure in any area?" How many times has a disempowering or judgmental word from someone, an act of pain from another person or even my lack of understanding on this important subject robbed me of my ability to move forward?

Stop for a moment and think about the things you wish you had never done, or the things that have happened to you that brought pain, and consider if you, in any way, have become frozen at that point. Maybe someone failed you and the pain of that still exists so you decided that you would never trust someone like that again. Or maybe the pain of your own failure has caused you to become stuck in that area. Fearing failure to the point of being paralysed will affect every area of life – from being able to see the will of God in the first place, to rising into all that He has planned for us. We can freeze at the point of failure in any area – physical, emotional, relational, mental or spiritual – especially where there is unaddressed pain.

DEFROSTING THE FREEZE

So, how can we override the freeze of failure? How can we stop freezing when we fail and, instead, begin to learn and move forward from our failures? For me, one of the great chapters in the Bible is 1 Corinthians 13. This chapter is known as the love chapter but it contains so much more than a simple love message:

Love never fails. But where there are prophecies, they will cease; where there are tongues, they will be stilled; where there is knowledge, it will pass away. For we know in part and we prophesy in part, but when completeness comes, what is in part disappears. When I was a child, I talked like a child, I thought like a child, I reasoned like a child. When I became a man, I put the ways of childhood behind me. For now we see only a reflection as in a mirror; then we shall see face to face.

Now I know in part; then I shall know fully, even as I am fully known. And now these three remain: faith, hope and love. But the greatest of these is love. 1 Corinthians 13:8–13 NIV

What I love about this scripture is that it assures us that we will fail! In fact, some translations render the word 'cease' with 'fail', bringing the understanding that whatever passes through a human form will never be completely perfect. We are all subject to failure, yet God's love will never fail us, even in the middle of our ongoing frailties.

God's love has never been conditional on human success

The Apostle Paul then continues on with a most freeing truth that so many of us are yet to capture. That truth is that, on this side of heaven, we know only 'in part'. We see only a little of the whole picture and we certainly don't know everything. Paul explains that, when we were children, we lived and responded as children. Too often, I have heard this verse interpreted only as we need to grow up. I believe that is true but there is a lot more to it than that. I believe Paul was also saying that, when we were children, we simply believed but, when we matured, we tried to work it all out and, when we couldn't, we stopped trying. God Himself doesn't expect us to know everything. As we mature, we often place an expectation of perfection on ourselves and those around us. Yet, Paul tells us that we still 'know in part' only and we will not fully understand everything until we reach eternity. God's ways are higher than our ways and people who know only in part are going to fail something, or somewhere, or sometime. I am not for a moment suggesting that we are not to reach for the best we can be and excuse our failures but, instead, that God understands our human frailties and we need to understand and accept them as well.

The lie that often seems to come into our thinking is that a day will come when we will arrive; we simply won't fail anymore. And yes, it is a lie. On this side of heaven, we know only 'in part', even as adults. Personally, I believe that the day will never come on earth when we stop failing.

Failure is the inevitable by-product of not knowing everything

Paul goes on to encourage us that faith, hope and love are what will remain. God encourages us to be people of faith, as faith pleases Him. Faith causes us to be people of committed action. It puts us into the realm of the impossible, the supernatural, where we are empowered to change because of His power within us, not in our own strength. The message that came through Paul 2000 years ago is still a relevant message from God's heart to ours today. He wants to teach us to live by faith and to take hold of our supernatural heritage. We will be able to address our frozen failure areas only with a spirit of faith.

Then God says that we are to live in the spirit of hope. No matter what we are faced with, we are to hope for a better tomorrow. We are to decide that, tomorrow, we will attempt to walk again. A resolute hope helps to aid the thawing process and to trust in a God who will walk beside us as that process takes place.

Finally, Paul writes, "*The greatest of these is love.*" The Apostle Paul understood the quality of God's love. He knew that the love that is God, never fails. This is a powerful kind of love. It is agape love. Agape love is amazing as it is not a selfish love… not the love that says, "I will love you when you begin to love me" or "I will love you if you are perfect and never fail". It is God-love. It is the love that will give without needing to receive anything in return: the love that covers our failures with His grace. Through Paul, God speaks to us, asking us to respond to this powerful love and to reach beyond where we have been before.

As we begin to understand failure, we understand that it is our dependence on God in faith, hope and love that is our true strength.

When we combine faith, hope and love, we find strength in failure

Instead of running and hiding, we can face failure and allow what was frozen and locked away in the freezer to begin to thaw. We can learn to overcome this failure freeze: to no longer limit our lives because of either the fear of failure or the actual failure. We can learn to see failure as an incredible asset, to see it as a pathway towards our learning and a greater future.

Let faith, hope and God's love arise in your heart as we continue in this book to delve into the effects failure has had on our thoughts, beliefs and actions.

KEY SCRIPTURE

1 Corinthians 13:8–13

REFLECTION

- In which personal areas can you identify failure freeze in your life (e.g. emotional, vocational, physical, spiritual)?
- What are some of the thoughts around the failure that have caused you to shut down and not process that failure?
- Take a moment to pray and ask God for help to face and process the pain, disappointment or guilt associated with failure, as you continue to read through the chapters of this book.

PRAYER

Lord, will you show me specific examples in my past where I have been frozen by failure? Father, please help me to dig deep and get to the root of it. Show me the depth of Your love for me, so I can move beyond those past experiences and break free into *failure freedom.*

GOD UNDERSTANDS

CHAPTER TWO

Failure is the only opportunity to begin again,
only this time more wisely.
Henry Ford

I have the privilege of travelling all over the world and find myself regularly speaking to people who desire so much more in their spiritual growth. A commonly asked question is: "What are some of the keys you know today, that you didn't know when you began your life and ministry journey?"

As I seek to answer that question, I find myself drifting so often to the matter of failure and the vital need to gain a God perspective on it. In thinking back on my own journey, there was something no one ever talked about that, had I understood, I believe would have added so much more potential and success to my life. What was never talked about was the absolute reality of failure in a Christian's life: the fact that every human being, while reaching for something greater and stretching for the best, will consistently experience failure. I never really heard or understood that God was with me, not just in strength, but also in weakness.

I'M A CHRISTIAN SO I SHOULDN'T FAIL, RIGHT?

I believe that the major key in releasing freedom for those caught by failure freeze is the simple realization that, because we are all human beings, failure is going to be a part of our lives, always.

According to the Bible, although we come into this world with unbelievable potential, created in the image of God, the truth of God's word is that we are also in a fallen world. Added to this is the fact that we carry around a sin nature that needs to be constantly surrendered to Christ.

Failure remains the staple diet of human advancement

As a result, we all are exposed to ongoing levels of failure, both our own failure and the failure of others. In fact, what I have come to discover is that the more committed we are to progressing forward, the more exposed we will be to failure.

Satan was created originally as a heavenly being with a purpose of worship and yet, like every human, had been given a free will. According to scripture, Satan chose to go against God, and his sin and rejection of God caused him to become an enemy of God's plans and purposes. We need to be very clear that Satan is not for us. He is against us. His sole purpose is to *steal and kill and destroy (John 10:10)*. He imposes his flawed and failure-ridden will on us and the environment in which we live.

I have been a Christian for most of my life and can't remember a time when I didn't love God and didn't want to live for Him with everything within me. As a young person, I wanted to give God my best and, to me, that meant I never wanted to fail along the way.

I grew up in a healthy family and was very engaged in a rich church environment where most of my memories were positive. I was taught to believe the best and bring my best because God was worth everything, and I wanted His best at whatever cost. Added to this, I was in a genuinely supernatural environment where we saw the unexpected take place on almost a weekly basis in church. It was amazing to see the lives that were turned around and the freedom that a relationship with God brought, let alone the many spiritual, emotional and, at times, physical miracles I saw. God could and would do what He said He would do. There was no doubt in my mind or my heart; my faith worked!

There was a serious flaw in my thinking, however. I believed that the more committed I was to the right things and the more obedient I was to the will of God, the less I would fail. You may have found you carry this same belief yourself. You believe that, because you are sold out to God, committed to His purposes in your life and obedient to what He is asking you to do, you will never experience failure.

What I discovered, however, was that this is not correct theology. Built into the positive perspective of our Christianity was a complete lack of teaching on the ability to handle failure. After all, we were never going to fail if we were being obedient to God… or were we? We had all sold out for God and He would always come through for us exactly as we expected Him to, wouldn't He? To fail or to miss the mark somehow meant we had lost our way.

The problem with this thinking is that, when we did fail, we didn't know what to do, except to take our foot off the accelerator and give up; seldom, or at times never, did we try what we had failed at again. Failure had little-to-no room in our thinking.

After many years of living with this misunderstanding on failure, I can say categorically that too many of us have an unrealistic image of what the Christian life is all about. Too many of us hit roadblocks created by this unrealistic view that we will never fail. We think that we must be able to reach our God-given dreams without failing, because, surely, if they are given by God, they won't involve failure. Then, when we fail, our lack of understanding about that failure creates a freeze moment, a roadblock, even a disappointment in or bitter root against God, rather than a lesson to a whole new highway of living.

Failing to understand failure creates a roadblock

GOD'S PERSPECTIVE

The Bible is full of people failing: left, right and centre! Right at the beginning in Genesis, we find Adam and Eve failing at living out God's command not to eat from the tree of knowledge of good and evil (Genesis 2:17). As we follow the story, we see God's chosen people, the Israelites, experiencing one failure after another. Even when Jesus enters the scene in the New Testament, failure doesn't take a break. Instead, failure is present in every person's journey of moving forward. Whether it was Peter denying Jesus three times, Paul persecuting Christians or Thomas doubting, the Bible is full of failure. What is fantastic, though, is that failure is not the end of their stories.

God delights in restoring and redeeming our failure for His glory

---

Take a look at Jesus' response to Peter's failure and see that, even after Peter failed Jesus by denying Him three times, Jesus renewed His calling and secured His position:

So when they had eaten breakfast, Jesus said to Simon Peter, "Simon, son of Jonah, do you love Me more than these?"

He said to Him, "Yes, Lord; You know that I love You."
He said to him, "Feed My lambs."
He said to him again a second time, "Simon, son of Jonah, do you love Me?"

He said to Him, "Yes, Lord; You know that I love You."
He said to him, "Tend My sheep."
He said to him the third time, "Simon, son of Jonah, do you love Me?"
Peter was grieved because He said to him the third time, "Do you love Me?"
And he said to Him, "Lord, You know all things; You know that I love You."
Jesus said to him, "Feed My sheep.
John 21:15–17 NKJV

We can only imagine how awkward Peter now felt being with Jesus. Where he had once been secure and self-assured as a close disciple, he now is before Jesus as one who had failed Him so miserably. Self-confidence and faith had withered to self-doubt and a feeling of being an utter failure. But Jesus wasn't just repeating Himself by asking this question three times; Jesus was being compassionate and loving. He was renewing Peter's calling and faith in himself. In the passage that follows, as Jesus described Peter's death, He was telling Peter that he would go on to be a man of great faith, the man that He believed he was.

For every failure in the lives of people in the Bible, there is a God who is constantly in the process of taking human failure and redeeming it into something life-giving.

God takes our failure and redeems it into something life-giving

---

When we do not have a correct failure theology, we so easily become trapped in failure. A repetitive cycle of trying something and failing continues to make us feel bad and, as a consequence, allows condemnation to grow. Ultimately, the pain of regret begins to dominate our lives. For each one of us, the load of unprocessed failure can become a weight that affects not only how we feel, but the speed at which we approach our future.

As I have mentioned, I grew up in a strong church environment. I can remember, however, in my early secondary school years, mixing with a group of guys who were far from God. The need to find acceptance caused me to compromise, particularly in the area of swearing. I remember battling with the condemnation as soon as a wrong word came out of my mouth. The condemnation was so strong that I feared I would be left behind if the second coming took place! Every Sunday, the first thing I would do is say sorry to God because I feared the outcome. It is true that sin separates us from God but it is also true that condemnation has the power to ensnare us. It was only when I realized that God knew and understood my battle and I could repent the moment it happened, that I gained the ability to overcome its power.

The outcome the enemy seeks for all of us is to become trapped within this continuous merry-go-round of failure because we have no understanding of how to deal with it, nor any understanding of how to create stepping-stones out of what we experience.

I believe too many of us are not living in freedom today because we are living under the domination of failure. The enemy's lies about failure, along with our own shame and disappointment, have continued to freeze us from moving forward. We are bound to old realities and our lack of understanding of those realities has continued to trap us. God longs to release us all into His 'now', freeing us from the bondage intended by Satan and into what He has for us. He has the ability, through His truth and love, to thaw those frozen places in our lives and cause us to want to step out again.

Newsflash – **God fully understands failure.** I am not for a moment saying that God condones sin, as sin separates us from Him. The kind of failure I am talking about is when we go through unexpected challenges and disappointments or the many times we don't achieve what we set out to achieve. God understands and has a way through these situations. In fact, He often does not shield us from these failures because of the powerful nature of their positive effects in our life. Failure, once processed correctly, is so powerful in unlocking potential.

When failure happens, we shouldn't pull back but should allow those times, experiences and situations to become building blocks for our future. Remember that God, because He knows and understands us, has allowed failure to be part of everyone's journey here on earth.

As we begin to seek a way forward, one insight that becomes crucial is that it is not the level of failure we experience, nor the failure imposed on us from others, it is our response to those failures that will be the key.

Failure, once processed, unlocks potential

As we continue to understand failure better, we won't waste so much time trying to dodge and avoid it but, rather, we will understand and embrace it, and increase in our ability to learn from it.

Ultimately, once understood and responded to correctly, failure can become the fuel used to free us to an enlarged future. To move forward into that future, we must continue to delve into the effects failure has had on our thoughts, beliefs and actions.

Welcome to the human race – failure is a human certainty!

KEY SCRIPTURE

John 21:15–17

REFLECTION

- Identify those beliefs and perspectives you hold that don't match up with what God thinks about failure.
- Identify any areas where you are stuck in a cycle of shame or condemnation about your ongoing failures. Commit to processing those thoughts and feelings with the truth of God's word.

PRAYER

Lord, help me to understand failure from Your perspective. Show me where I have an incorrect view of You and Your Word. Father, help me to know who I am as a child of God and who You have called me to be, so that I no longer suffer under the power of condemnation but, instead, rise to that calling, as Peter did, with a joy and security that is firmly rooted in You.

LASTING ECHOES

CHAPTER THREE

You build on failure. You use it as a stepping-stone. Close the door on the past. You don't try to forget the mistakes, but you don't dwell on it. You don't let it have any of your energy, or any of your time, or any of your space.

Johnny Cash

Have you ever found yourself dominated by an internal voice that continues to remind you of something in your past that you would rather forget about? When we fail at something, what so often happens is that we continue to live in the misery of an internal conversation that feeds us with lies such as: "I knew it wouldn't work; I should never have tried that in the first place. From now on, I am not going to risk it. I just haven't got it; I really knew that at the start." What this internal voice does is try to attach the failure of our past into our present. The echoes of past failure, when not dealt with, try to hold us back from moving forward into our future.

Many years ago, when pastoring at Hillsong Church in Sydney, I was asked to visit a man who was in prison. I was surprised to meet a very quietly spoken man, who, after a few visits, began to open up a little about the trauma of his past. Jim (not his real name) had served his nation as a Green Beret (a highly skilled soldier) in Vietnam.

Unfortunately, the events that happened during his time in the military had severely impacted who he was and his ability to live as an everyday citizen. After I had visited this man many times, we formed a strong connection and relationship, and, after his release, he agreed to come to church with me.

I will never forget the first Sunday he came along. He was very much on edge and just being amongst a crowd of people made him feel nervous. Not long after the service started, he ran out of the building. I followed him, found him, and we sat together and had a coffee. He explained to me that he felt severely shaken, as he found himself thinking he was back in the Vietnamese jungle, where every noise presented potential danger.

The echoes of Jim's past were still the loudest voices in his mind, even though he was no longer in that place of danger. Because of these echoes of the past, he was unable to make new steps in the present and towards his future. Jim was obviously experiencing a high level of trauma but what struck me was the power of the echo in his world. The same is true with failure; the echoes of our past can wield significant power over us if they are not dealt with and processed correctly.

The echoes of our past have the power to paralyse us

THE POWER OF THE ECHO

An echo is a reflection of an original sound that arrives at the listener some time after the direct sound is made. In the context of failure, it is a combination of the ongoing thoughts and feelings that continue to come to mind, long after that failure has passed. An echo usually would be weaker in sound than was the original; however, if the feelings and emotions around failure remain unprocessed, that echo can, at times, increase in volume and continue to echo on and on in our hearts and minds. When we try to move forward or start something new, those thoughts and emotions seem to jump out from nowhere with great intensity, determined to hold us back. We can call into a cave and hear: "Hello, hello, hello... "; similarly, the echo of failure can call: "Don't try again, don't try again, don't try again... ". Effectively, the echoes of failure can paralyse us and stop us from stepping out and moving forward.

Just as failure is a human condition that we all face, so the echoes of failure are something we all have to deal with, too. You would think that the more mature a person is, the less this issue of failure would be true; however, the more we step out, the more we will fail.

I have been pastoring now for well in excess of 30 years and have connections and relationships with pastors and leaders all over the world. I often receive phone calls from different ones, each telling me about something that is going wrong in their world. In a funny kind of way, that is encouraging because I hear the echo of failure that I have so often heard coming from within myself.

Our freedom is not when we cease to hear the echoes of failure; it is when we commit to ignore them and move past them and so reduce their volume and impact on us. Every one of us has the sound of failure attached to our journey and, the more quickly we realize it and bring it out into the open, the sooner we will walk free. With God's grace, we can embrace the lessons failure brings to us, and that will enable us to reach new levels of freedom.

Our freedom is found when we replace the voice of the past with the promise of the future

---

CHALLENGING THE ECHO

King David is a stunning example of someone processing failure and moving forward, rather than allowing the echoes of failure to dominate his life. David – probably the greatest king of history – was described as a man after God's heart. He had a relationship with God that was breathtaking; however, he was also an adulterer and a premeditated murderer. What I love about David is his transparency with God after his failures. He does not hide, or freeze, or make excuses. He cries out to God and allows God to take him on a journey of processing his failure and moving forward.

David wrote in Psalm 51:3 NIV:

For I know my transgressions, and my sin is always before me.

Then, to emphasize the point, he continued in verse 5:

Surely I was sinful at birth, sinful from the time my mother conceived me.

David realized that his humanity was part of him. When he sinned on a grand scale, instead of freezing (the ultimate failure, I think), he turned to the wonder of God's grace and cried out: *Create in me a pure heart, O God, and renew a steadfast spirit within me (Psalm 51:10 NIV).* David didn't make excuses; he owned that he had failed and that he was not able to do and be everything that was needed of him to live in perfection. His failure, followed by his cry of honest repentance, accessed God's grace and became the foundation point for his future.

We stand, live and operate by that same wonder of the grace of God. You see, moving closer to God does not mean the elimination of failure. In fact, it can heighten the reality of failure! The closer to Him we are, the more we see our weaknesses and frailties and the more we have a decision to make, and that is to embrace the ability to process failure.

David deliberately exposed his failure and, therefore, allowed God to listen to the sound of his failure. That's what we need to do too. Rather than hiding the failure and succumbing to the echoes, we must expose our failures to God and allow His grace to come into those areas.

The ability to process failure is a decision we get to make

THE POWER OF GRACE

James writes in James 3:2,

For we all stumble in many things.

Then, as if to emphasize the point, he adds:

If anyone does not stumble in word, he is a perfect man, able also to bridle the whole body.

I have yet to meet that man or woman who can honestly say that they have total mastery of their life: words, attitudes, behaviour. It is true that this is to be our goal – to have our inner world aligned with God's standards of righteous living. But the pathway is that we all stumble in many ways.

The writer to the very immature church in Rome encouraged the people with this teaching:

For all have sinned and fall short of the glory of God, being justified freely by his grace through the redemption that is in Christ Jesus. Romans 3:23–24

Here is the picture that the writer was painting. We wake up in the morning and ready ourselves for the race of life. We stand on the starting line, the gun goes off and we start running. Things are looking good… we are in front! Suddenly, however, we trip on something and see the ground coming up towards us. We fall. We fail.

Lifting our eyes from the dirt and grit, we find that everyone else is miles in front; at that point, we so often freeze. The pain and shame of the fall, and the reality of the unexpected challenge, echo in our mind and heart. We have fallen short of the goal. We are left behind. It is a miserable moment. At that point, we ask ourselves: "Is it worth getting up?"

But then the grace of God visits us. If we choose to accept His help, He does not leave us alone on the track and He does not leave us where we are. If our failure is due to sin, He offers forgiveness; if it is simply a mistake, then there is the opportunity of a life lesson. In an instant, He picks us up from the very point of stumbling and, through His strength and His ability, leads us onward. However, He doesn't just put us back into the race; He repositions us back at the front of the race. You see, the falling and failing are not the point. The point is this – that our falling and failure introduces us to the grace of God and, in that, is the wonder of it all – the awesome wonder of His grace.

Our failure always introduces us to the grace of God

Growth in God is not the avoidance of failure. In fact, when we spend so much time trying to avoid failure, we end up living in a very small and tightly controlled world. Instead, when we fail, we encounter the lavish, unending grace of God. When we choose to access His truth and empowerment, we are able to leave the echoes of failure behind and step forward into the freedom that God has for us.

KEY SCRIPTURE

Romans 3:23–24

REFLECTION

- Which situations echo loudest with regard to your past failures? Identify which ones condemn you and commit to bringing them to God and leaving them with Him.
- How can you challenge the echoes of failure in your own life?
- Do you have any areas which you need to process through the filter of God's grace?

PRAYER

Lord, search my heart right now and show me… show me the power of Your grace, Father, and teach me how to receive it into every area of my heart that has grown cold and dead from those haunting echoes. I choose to believe Your word over the lies and echoes of my past.

GRANDSTAND LIVING

CHAPTER FOUR

Far better it is to dare mighty things, to win glorious triumphs, even though checkered by failure, than to rank with those timid spirits who neither enjoy nor suffer much because they live in the gray twilight that knows neither victory nor defeat.

Theodore Roosevelt

I remember, in my early teenage years, having a strong desire to play a musical instrument. I had a younger brother who was extremely gifted in the area of music and I would watch him play the drums with amazing ability, and then the guitar, and finally the bass, which became his instrument of choice. I remember trying to play the drums when no one was around, trying to make both hands and feet work in unison. I must have managed to coordinate my limbs to some extent as I was asked to play at a very small event. Unfortunately, I made such a hash of it that I never picked up the drumsticks again!

The echoes of failure, if not processed, end up causing us to live a risk-averse life. As we have already seen, failure becomes a problem when we allow it to freeze us at the point of the failure. When we do this, we attach our present and future to something in our past. We enter a time warp. Something inside of us fails to grow and so we become distorted in how we see life, in how we see ourselves and in our willingness to get up to try again.

We usually refuse to have another go at what we failed to succeed in. We allow failure to reduce us to a future of decreasing risk and ultimate inactivity. We allow the potholes on the road to our future to cause us to take a detour or, worse, a complete stop. We would achieve so much more if we worked through our failures to a place where we were willing, once again, to take a risk.

The residue of failure can cause us to live a risk-averse life

---

Theodore Roosevelt was the 26th president of the United States of America. In a speech, entitled Citizenship in a Republic, given at the Sorbonne in Paris on 23 April 1910, he uttered these famous and stirring words:

It is not the critic who counts: not the man who points out how the strong man stumbles or where the doer of deeds could have done better. The credit belongs to the man who is actually in the arena, whose face is marred by dust and sweat and blood, who strives valiantly, who errs and comes up short again and again, because there is no effort without error or shortcoming … but who knows the great enthusiasms, the great devotions, who spends himself for a worthy cause; who, at the best, knows, in the end, the triumph of high achievement, and who, at the worst, if he fails, at least he fails while daring greatly, so that his place shall never be with those cold and timid souls who knew neither victory nor defeat.

It is not uncommon for our failures to make us feel silly, embarrassed or even stupid for ever having believed that we could achieve what we had attempted in the first place. How often have we heard the phrase: "I just wanted the earth to open up and swallow me"? Failure wants us to run and hide: to take ourselves out of the game. The problem is that, when we do that, sure, we don't experience the defeat but neither do we experience the success. If we never move from the grandstand, if we allow our past failures to keep us from ever trying again, we will receive neither the joy of success nor even the satisfaction of knowing we gave it our best shot. A grandstand mentality also creates a dangerous attitude within us that Roosevelt also mentions – that when living a risk-averse life due to failure, we often end up judging those who are actually out there having a go.

FAILURE AND JUDGMENT

I once went to watch a rugby game – one of New Zealand's favourite pastimes. I was astounded at the level of criticism and judgment spouting forth from the mouth of one of the spectators standing close to me. Every time a tackle was missed or a ball was dropped, there were so many ugly words being shouted at those on the field, it was appalling: words such as, "what an idiot!" and "you're useless!" At one point on this bitterly cold Saturday morning, I felt like turning around and saying, "Why don't you get down there and see if you can do it any better?"

Why is it, as human beings, we feel the need to so quickly point out the failures of those who are actually attempting something? Why is it that, even within the Church, many are happier to take seats within the protection and comfort of the grandstand and engage in judging others through the pointing of their own inactive fingers at those who fail while trying to achieve something? At the very least, they are prepared to get out onto the field and have a go.

Taking that further, I think that the stance of criticism often comes about because of an individual's inability to face their own failures and this results in an over-projection of judgment on those prepared to take risks.

We all have experienced the effect of criticism coming from the voice of the crowd so let's all ensure we don't become part of that group. The 'crowd' may be a parent, or a teacher, or a few school bullies, or a workmate or even a spouse; it doesn't matter. That one person or group of people, who made us feel rotten at some past time in our lives, fills the stands. If we fail to guard against the voice of doubt, it may become the most dominant voice we hear and end up as criticism and derision into our soul.

It doesn't stop there. All of us can end up choosing to do life from the stands as it can so easily become a place to retreat to: a place where we no longer take the risks which carry the possibility of failure. Somehow, to validate our own frozen state, our own paralysis, it seems easier to judge others who seem to be living in freedom.

Once frozen by failure, our judgment of others can increase

The Bible is clear about the matter of judgment. We are not to stand in judgment over anyone or anything to which we are not able to bring healing or change.

But why do you judge your brother? Or why do you show contempt for your brother? For we shall all stand before the judgment seat of Christ. For it is written: " As I live, says the Lord, Every knee shall bow to Me, And every tongue shall confess to God." So then each of us shall give account of himself to God. Therefore let us not judge one another anymore, but rather resolve this, not to put a stumbling block or a cause to fall in our brother's way. Romans 14:10–13

The Bible tells us that, at the end of time, we will all stand before God and that He will ask us what we did with our own life, not with someone else's.

When we see people going through situations that look like failure, let's never forget what it felt like when we tripped up or were faced with an embarrassing failure; just as we longed for mercy and understanding in our dark time, so we ought also to give mercy and understanding to others.

Ultimately, to live past the echoes of failure and embrace a life of stepping out in faith, the voice of truth must come to us. Jesus said: *I am the way, THE TRUTH, and the life (John 14:6*). He is our truth: the voice that will encourage us to keep going and keep trusting and keep believing. Fantastic examples of believing the voice of truth and stepping out in faith are found in Hebrews 11, 'the faith chapter', but one of my favourites is Abraham.

Our world needs a growing number of people who will venture from the safe zone of a low-risk attitude: people who are willing to tap into the security of God's love and believe in the final outcome of an enlarged future as Abraham did. Because of his faith, confronting all of the odds, he became a father of many nations (Romans 4:17–18).

You and I are to be those people. I do not want to be part of a life or belong to a church that is paralysed by a sense of past failure. "Well, that didn't work so let's stop trying." The world does not need a church that no longer attempts the impossible! It needs a church that understands the freeing, even healthy, nature of failure.

We must no longer allow failure to take the position of Lord in our lives. We must choose to move out of the grandstands and onto the field. We must continue to embrace the pathway of risk and all that comes with it, including the failure.

**If we allow failure to remain unchallenged,
we allow it room to control**

And as we do, we can rest in the knowledge that we have a God who promises to uphold us and help us back onto the pathway of success.

We fall, we fail but we are not cast down. We get up. We keep on trying because we have this hope found in scripture:

And I am convinced and sure of this very thing, that He Who began a good work in you will continue until the day of Jesus Christ [right up to the time of His return], developing [that good work] and perfecting and bringing it to full completion in you. Philippians 1:6 AMP

KEY SCRIPTURE

Romans 14:10–13

REFLECTION

- Where do you have a risk-averse attitude? Identify any areas in your life in which you are living 'in the grandstands' rather than out on the field.
- Are you judging others who are out having a go because it makes you feel better about not trying?
- How have your previous failures affected your views on trying again or stepping out and what do you need to do to change these views?

PRAYER

Lord, I long to live a life free from the fear of failure that holds me back from a life full of faith and excitement. Please show me and forgive me if I have been living in judgment of others. Today, I ask You to help me no longer to live life in the stands but, instead, give me the courage to move forward to the abundant life that You have promised to give me.

FAILURE FREEDOM

PART TWO

MY OTHER ME

CHAPTER FIVE

Success is the ability to go from failure to failure without losing your enthusiasm.
Winston Churchill

As we have seen, failure can manifest itself in so many different ways. I want to focus now on how we move towards failure freedom – a life where we can feel free to move forward, embracing failure as a pathway for success.

The whole Christian message shouts out the truth that God understands failure, uses failure and forgives failure when it comes to sin. And yet the whole plan of Satan is to keep us constantly entangled by failure. Every good thing that God brings to us will be met by a counter-plan that is deviously and cruelly thought up by our enemy. Without even realizing it, we can respond to failure as those who are entangled, rather than those who are forgiven; we can respond as people who have no choice but to give up after failure, rather than those who have been set free to stand tall and continue on.

In Christ, freedom awaits on the other side of failure

Most Christians reading this book will know with their head that Jesus forgives all of our failures and that His intention is for us to move forward past failure, but somehow the power and pull of failure can override any ability we have to live free from it.

Here is the best explanation I can give about that irony. I'd like you to picture a set of twins living inside each of us – the redeemed and spiritual twin who is set free from sin and failure, and the twin whose natural habitat is carnality.

One of the most outstanding chapters in the entire book of Romans and, in fact, the whole New Testament is the revelation that the Apostle Paul brought to the New Testament church in Romans 7:

For we know that the law is spiritual, but I am carnal, sold under sin. For what I am doing, I do not understand. For what I will to do, that I do not practice; but what I hate, that I do. If, then, I do what I will not to do, I agree with the law that it is good. But now, it is no longer I who do it, but sin that dwells in me. For I know that in me (that is, in my flesh) nothing good dwells; for to will is present with me, but how to perform what is good I do not find. For the good that I will to do, I do not do; but the evil I will not to do, that I practice. Now if I do what I will not to do, it is no longer I who do it, but sin that dwells in me. I find then a law, that evil is present with me, the one who wills to do good. For I delight in the law of God according to the inward man. But I see another law in my members, warring against the law of my mind, and bringing me into captivity to the law of sin which is in my members. O wretched man that I am! Who will deliver me from this body of death? I thank God – through Jesus Christ our Lord! So then, with the mind I myself serve the law of God, but with the flesh the law of sin. Romans 7:14–25

There it is. We can know truth in our heads but, deep in our hearts, we are still living in the grip of failure. We can know in our heads that God has forgiven past sin, mistakes and failures but, deep in our hearts, we are still quaking in fear at the thought of re-entering life.

Have you ever had someone say to you: "You are special; you are unique; you are the only one in the entire world with your fingerprint?" It is all so true, yet you have just read something quite confronting from Paul's pen. He teaches that our special and unique self is actually an encasing of two opposing forces. The self that delights in God's law is at war with the self that keeps us prisoner to sin.

When it comes to understanding the components of failure, it is this internal battle that is often the biggest battle of all.

The battleground of failure remains in our internal world

FEEDING THE RIGHT TWIN

When we begin our Christian walk, our born-again or redeemed self is small and does not yet have a lot of influence and strength over the carnal self that has been running our lives for many years.

We can go to church and feed our redeemed self. We can leave inspired to read our Bible and live for God: to make the changes we desperately want to make. We believe He has spoken to us and we are ready to let our redeemed self fly.

Somewhere on the way home, or the next day, however, we meet our carnal twin. It is bigger and stronger than we realized it was. Replay Romans 7. *What we want to do, we don't do; what we don't do, we should do.*

How do we respond? After all, this dual self drove Paul to say: *O wretched man that I am.* Romans 7:24.

Thankfully, God has given an amazing antidote to the battle further on in Romans:

There is therefore now no condemnation to those who are in Christ Jesus, who do not walk according to the flesh, but according to the Spirit. For the law of the Spirit of life in Christ Jesus has made me free from the law of sin and death. Romans 8:1–2

To the carnal, sinful self that wants to stay frozen in failure comes this truth that melts our cold and miserable hearts: we are not condemned.

Condemnation was not created by God and, therefore, we must not allow it room

---

We can, therefore, respond by declaring that we are not allowing the enemy to kill, steal from or destroy us. We declare that we will not give way to the lies of the enemy about who we are and about our failures.

And so the joyous and spiritual twin, the twin who desires to do all that God has called us to do, becomes not just the stronger twin but our identity in Christ.

Oh how I wish I had understood this as a young man. I grew up wanting to live a victorious Christian life. One part of me was ready to fly for God. The other part was always going to drift towards the low side of life – carnality. The 'ready to fly for God' twin found it nearly impossible to acknowledge this frail and human other half. I would fail and then, somehow, have to turn my back on the part of me that failed.

Now, no longer a young man, I have made a huge life change. I have given myself the freedom to fail.

Give yourself the freedom to fall short while reaching for something greater

This is not a perverse passion to sin, and not in any way an approval for any form of compromise of God's word and ways, but rather the freedom to embrace some new level of maturity or new understanding that God has for me when I fail. I have taken the internal fight away. By the wonder of God's grace, I have weakened the internal twin that kept me in a cycle of sin and condemnation.

Once I recognized that there were two of me slugging it out on the inside, I began to feed my spiritual self and starve my carnal self. While I am alive, that carnal self is going to have enough kick to make me fail at times, while I am trying to succeed. The failures – mistakes and sins of the past – threaten me constantly but what I don't do any longer is deny that my other me exists. I am going to fail. I will not let it take me out; I will confine it, keep trying and move on.

Even though mistakes and failures occur, the 'other twin' must never dictate the way we walk before God. We walk before Him as those who are not condemned. The truth is that the Holy Spirit convicts us of sin and wrong and leads us to repentance, which releases God's forgiveness, but He never condemns us. Condemnation is the trap of failure that has no key that fits the lock. The carnal twin does not draw God's attention and is not His way of escape. God sees us as covered in the robe of righteousness and, therefore, wants us to live in Him beyond the lie and limitation of condemnation.

We must learn to confine these unredeemed parts of us that would cause us to continue to live frozen by failure and bound to the past. Along with that, we must build up and strengthen our redeemed self, including our thoughts and beliefs surrounding that part of us. It is these skills that we will now turn towards discussing, as we move towards failure freedom.

KEY SCRIPTURE

Romans 7:14–25

REFLECTION

- In which areas can you identify the battle of the twins inside you?
- How can you build strength in the redeemed part of you to see breakthrough and forward movement in areas of weakness?
- What are some verses in scripture that speak about your identity in Christ? Write them down and speak them out loud when 'the other twin's' voice is loudest.

PRAYER

Father, show me how to put to death the fleshly side of me. Help me to walk more in the Spirit each day, pursuing my identity in You. For you have made me a new creation and the old things have passed away. Teach me how to take every thought captive to the obedience of Christ. Lord, I declare that I am Yours and I submit my will to You.

FENCING FAILURE

CHAPTER SIX

Develop success from failures. Discouragement and failure are two of the surest stepping-stones to success.
Dale Carnegie

One way to confine something is to put a fence around it. Having emphasized the inevitability of failure and the consequences of not dealing with our failures, there is now a very important action for us to take if we want to live in the fullness of our faith. We must learn to put boundaries and fences around our failures to thereby confine them to their rightful place. If it is sin, then the forgiveness for which Jesus has already paid must be applied. If the failure is in not achieving what we had hoped to achieve, we must get back up and run again, no matter how often we have fallen short.

Such boundaries will help us rise again after a failure and help us fight against those thoughts and feelings, which tempt us to give up. When we set up those boundaries and fight this battle, we must remember what Paul wrote:

The weapons we fight with are not the weapons of the world. On the contrary, they have divine power to demolish strongholds. We demolish arguments and every pretension that sets itself up against the knowledge of God, and ***we take captive every thought to make it obedient to Christ.*** 2 Corinthians 10:4–5 NIV (emphasis added)

Also, remember that the battle is in the mind, which is why we are taking the thoughts captive; it is a spiritual battle, so be aggressive, bring out that inner warrior and put on your armour as it instructs us to do in Ephesians.

Put on the full armor of God, so that you can take your stand against the devil's schemes. For our struggle is not against flesh and blood, but against the rulers, against the authorities, against the powers of this dark world and against the spiritual forces of evil in the heavenly realms. Ephesians 6:11–12 NIV

Visualize yourself doing this if that helps to set those fences and boundaries around your past failures.

When we don't put boundaries around our failures, they threaten to take our future territory and seek to become a pattern of repeated failure.

When we don't fence our failures,
they threaten to fence our future

As a young man, I loved to windsurf. Some 10 years later, after not having windsurfed much at all, I had an opportunity to go with a friend who was one of the best windsurfers around and had been sailing his whole life. I wasn't kidding myself about my lack of condition but I was keen to be out on the water again.

The wind was up. I was on a board that was more hi-tech than my old one had been; the sails had the right tension (not like the old ones that used to rattle around), everything was prepared and he said,

"Let's go".

It wasn't long before I found myself actually in the water more than I was on the board! This went on for what seemed like an eternity but may have been only about 30 minutes.

A windsurfer comes with a harness, which is the key to taking the strain that comes from the sail through your arms, and transferring the speed to the board you are standing on. Without it, you blow your forearms out and all strength abates very quickly. I wasn't using a harness as I was unable to get everything working the way I used to; finally, I had to admit I was in big trouble. My muscles, through overuse, were exploding and I was not enjoying myself at all. I wanted to succeed so much; I so clearly remembered being able to windsurf and the incredible feeling that comes with flying over the water at great speed, and yet, the harder I tried, the more frustrating it seemed to become.

I was utterly exhausted already and we had barely left the beach. My old, familiar friend 'failure' began to echo: "You won't be able to make it; you should just give up now". I decided, however, to push through and to try to use the harness. A harness positions you to pick up any gust of wind and move forward, relying on the balance of your body weight rather than the strength of your arms. Just as well, as my arm strength at this point was non-existent!

Once engaged in the harness, I then discovered I wasn't positioned correctly and a gust of wind lifted me off the board and sent me crashing into the sail and the water. Instantly, I thought, "Jesus, I'm coming home!" It was a mess. Any ideas of impressing my friend were long gone. It was just me and Jesus… mostly Jesus!

Eventually, I was able to pull it together. The moment came when I chose to say, "Enough!" (I think the word 'enough' sounded more like "Jesus, help me… " but you get the point!) I managed to control my body and the windsurf board and went on to have a degree of success.

On reflection, I realized that the only way I was able to move from failure towards success was by putting boundaries around my sense of failure and reining it in. By rejecting the voice of failure and then taking steps towards success, I confined it. By being willing to change and use the right technique, even when that decision also led me to fail initially, I was able to embrace early failure and continue to use the harness; that meant that, eventually, I moved forward. It would have been so easy to give up but I was determined to fence in my failure and continue to move forward towards success.

FENCING THE PAST

To embrace and learn from failure is to move forward. Our ongoing challenge is not just to stop freezing at failure, but to confine it to the moment or season of the failure, and then ask what we can learn from it. Just because something doesn't initially work out, it doesn't mean it never will. We may need to add something or do something differently but, ultimately, every failure, when embraced, has a lesson for us to learn.

Confine your failure to the season of your failure

Therefore, we must put fences and boundaries around our failures so that they don't affect the next season of our life. We also need to make sure that we learn from our mistakes and use that knowledge towards our future success.

The writer of Proverbs describes this process in Proverbs 24:16 NIV: *For though a righteous man falls seven times, he rises again...*

The righteous man does not stay down. He confines failure to its rightful place and rises again. The same verse finishes with: ...but the wicked are brought down by calamity. The wicked man's failures are all out of order; they have no shape or boundary. He is just out of control.

God wants us to live beyond such chaos, even in our failures.

One of the greatest revelations I have had to learn is that failure exists only in the present tense. We can't change yesterday.

Failure exists only in the present tense

Even though we might do many things differently if we could, we can't go back. Things have happened and that is that. However, when we allow the shadow and ghost of those things of yesterday into today, we keep failure alive in our today.

Our unwillingness to put a boundary or fence around the past means that it has the right to enter our present. This results in failure living on into the present and the price for the failure continues to be paid. One of the great boundary lines of life that we can put in place is the one that goes something like this: "Yes, I have failed but the grace of God covers me in that failure. I now choose to move forward, learning from the past, into the future that God has for me. I refuse to let the ghost of my failure hold me back in my present and my future."

When we give God charge over our lives, His voice comes to us in our failure and says, "I am building something great in you and from your life". We can let Him know that we don't like the pain of the failure but we then must choose to cooperate with His bigger plans. God works in our today and tomorrow while the enemy wants us to continue in yesterday.

Failure reminds us that He is God and that we aren't. Yes, we are finite. Yes, we might sprawl in the mud or flap about under a windsurfer instead of riding it like a pro. We are finite. But when we lock into His infiniteness, He uses our failures to position us in strength and in His bigger, higher plans.

REQUIRED ACCOUNTABILITIES

Another way that we fence our failure is by having people in our lives who continue to push us forward and out of a failure mindset. Just as failure is a human condition that we all face, so too, the challenge of fencing failure is something we all have to deal with. Often, just understanding that others face the same things that we face can encourage our heart. The Bible puts it this way in 1 Peter 5:9 ISV (emphasis added)

Resist him [the devil] and be firm in the faith, ***because you know that your brothers throughout the world are undergoing the same kinds of suffering.***

In the same way, when we share our journey of failure with others, we bring them freedom and encouragement too:

As iron sharpens iron, so a friend sharpens a friend. Proverbs 27:17 NLT

A few years ago, our church staff had finished a very big season of activity and we wanted to take some time out to recharge our batteries. We spent time with God and time relaxing. One afternoon, staff members could choose their relaxation activities. Some shopped, some went paint-balling and some went moto-cross riding. My oldest son Luke and I, along with a few others, chose moto-cross riding.

So, we set off. Soon into the ride, we found some narrow tracks and decided to follow them up the mountain and into the bush. The track was steep in parts and quite wet and clayey. The bikes were slipping all over the place and it wasn't long before all of us had come off our bikes at least once. It was quite challenging. I loved it.

Luke, on the other hand, who was on his first-ever moto-cross ride, did not love it! He seemed to be coming off at just about every corner. There were lots of deep ruts and, if you slipped into them and relaxed, you could continue without coming off. If you tried to fight them, however, you would come off for sure.

I was saying to Luke, "Come on, you can do it. I'll wait for you. Just follow my tracks." But he just kept falling over and, like some of the other riders, ended up in a gorse bush. My encouragement wasn't very helpful as I continued: "God has a broad ministry for you, son!"

Finally, I told him to go ahead of me so that we could take it at his pace. The other riders had taken off and I didn't want him left too far behind. I was just a little behind him and rounding one of the corners when I saw Luke sprawled out all over the mud. It was everywhere. He was pounding the dirt in frustration. I said, "Hey, mate, it's your first time and this is not easy on wet clay." He responded, "No, it's not alright. I should be able to do this."

We picked up the bike, dug mud out of the wheels and then I asked Luke what he was doing down the hills. He told me that he was pulling the clutch in on the declines. Pulling the clutch in means the back wheel would need the brakes to be applied a lot more frequently and, therefore, would lock the tyres up, causing him to constantly fall off. But, by using the engine to help slow the bike down, he would not skid as much. I told him this and, fast learner that he is, Luke got back on the bike, took off and had a great day.

Here is the thought. Some of us never move past pounding the dirt. We aren't willing to ask for help; we aren't willing to humble ourselves or embarrass ourselves by admitting that it's just too hard for us. Those of us who can rein in failure have an attitude that we will no longer do life without help: that we will choose to follow the tracks that others have laid down before us in their wisdom and experience.

Failure freedom requires the humility to ask for help

Failure freedom requires that we are humble enough to ask for help, allowing others to act as boundary-markers for us. We can let people into our lives to challenge us in our failures, to encourage us to move forward and to check whether we are listening to the voice of failure or the voice of God.

Whether windsurfing, moto-crossing or just plain living, we won't move ahead unless we commit to fencing our failures: fence the thoughts and echoes that exist around them *(take every thought captive to the obedience of Christ* 2 Corinthians 10:5), fence the guilt and condemnation that tries to arise *(there is now no condemnation for those who are in Christ Jesus* Romans 8:1) and fence the internal twin that pulls us back towards our carnal nature *(you are a new creation in Christ* 2 Corinthians 5:17). We must fence the past and allow others to speak into our lives (*As iron sharpens iron, so a friend sharpens a friend* Proverbs 27:17). We must allow our failure to take us into a place of discovery and learning.

By the wonder of God's grace and our ability to fence our failures, those failures can then become stepping-stones to bigger and greater attempts at the possibilities of the life we have in Christ.

Forget the former things; do not dwell on the past. See, I am doing a new thing! Now it springs up; do you not perceive it? I am making a way in the wilderness and streams in the wasteland. Isaiah 43:18–19 NIV (emphasis added)

KEY SCRIPTURE

2 Corinthians 10:4–5

REFLECTION

- What are some ways by which you can learn to take your thoughts captive and put on your spiritual armour so you can put boundary markers around past failure?
- How can you bring others into your journey to help you fence your failure?
- What eternal fruit can you see emerging out of your failures as you continue to learn from them?

PRAYER

Father, teach me how to battle Your way. Show me how to 'suit up' in my spiritual armour and put boundaries around my past failures: how to stop dwelling on them and to lay hold of the new thing You are doing in me. Teach me to be expectant and hopeful about the possibilities and opportunities I have from a life spent with You.

EMBRACING FAILURE

CHAPTER SEVEN

I've missed more than 9000 shots in my career. I've lost almost 300 games. Twenty-six times I've been trusted to take the game-winning shot and missed. I've failed over and over and over again in my life. And that is why I succeed.

Michael Jordan

The story is told of a primary school teacher who regularly asked his class in an upbeat way: "How many mistakes have you made today?" The larger the number of unrepeated mistakes, the more enthusiastically he congratulated them, for that indicated how much the student had been prepared to go beyond the limits of their current existence to a greater place of learning.

That is the failure freedom message – to embrace learning, we must be secure enough to walk a failure pathway.

Learning is the primary purpose of failure

We must bring ourselves to a place where, instead of trying to avoid failure, we actually are able to embrace it as a pathway forward to greater success. I love these quotes about failure from successful leaders of the past:

"I have not failed. I've just found 10,000 ways that won't work." **Thomas Edison**

"There is no failure except in no longer trying." **Elbert Hubbard**

"Only those who dare to fail greatly can ever achieve greatly." **Robert Kennedy**

How powerful are these profound insights, coming from human beings committed to lives of unfolding potential? The common thread is that failure leads towards success and that failure spurs us on towards greatness but, ultimately, the greatest failure is when we stop trying. I am convinced that the graveyards of the world are filled with people who died living short of what could have been because they gave in to the lie that failure deserved to have the final say.

Ultimately, our greatest failure is if we fail to try again

On a visit to the USA many years ago, I had the opportunity to see my first American baseball game. It is an interesting game, full of statistics that mystified me. I have a real passion when it comes to sports and like to know how things work. So, at the game, I asked the person who had generously taken me along to explain what I didn't understand. While I was watching the game, up came this statistic – the batter who was facing the pitcher had a .367 average. I learned that this meant that, for every 1000 balls pitched to him, he had connected with 367 of them. Let me put that another way. This superstar batter, who in America was an all-time champion, had missed 633 times out of 1000 attempts! For every one ball that this athlete hit, he missed two, yet the crowd roared every time he came up to bat and he was paid multiple millions of dollars for every season he played. He was so admired that he was credited with bringing thousands to the grounds week after week. This man certainly understood the definition of enthusiastic failure – he had built a career out of it!

Isn't it amazing that often we expect a success rate of 10 out of 10 for ourselves? I totally believe in reaching for the best but also that every attempt has value if we see failure as a learning point. When we have to succeed on every attempt, we constantly put ourselves under unnecessary, and what I call, negative pressure. This baseball batter failed twice as often as he succeeded, yet he didn't allow what happened on the last attempt to limit his expectation for the next one. He continued to move forward and to risk failure again and, because of that, he saw great success in his chosen field. He had an internal marker that said, "That was not failure. That was just one swing that will eventuate in a sweet connection just around the corner."

What are your internal markers? Are they like those of this baseball batter? Do they mirror an ability to fail with a view to the future and knowledge of the learning attached to them?

BIBLICAL FAILURES

When we look to the Bible, I think it is too easy to live with a romantic picture of disciples and Biblical heroes. The truth is, the stories we have been given paint a very real picture of humanity.

Judas was a robber and continued to steal, even after three years of the best Bible College around. Ultimately, this flaw in his character led to his death. Peter cursed and denied Jesus, just after knifing a man in a park. Yet, he was arguably one of the three people who were closest to Jesus on an everyday basis. Thomas sat in on all of Jesus' lectures and still was plagued continually by doubt and distrust.

All three experienced failure; all three felt the internal pressure to give up, yet what is inspiring is that only Judas gave in to its call. The other two men were able to rise beyond their failures and continue to achieve great things for God.

Remember the illustration, found in the Gospels, of Jesus speaking to one very hungry crowd? Think of the little boy who looks at 5000 men, plus women and children, and says, "I think, with Jesus in the mix, my mum's given me enough food to go around". We don't know much about him but what we do see is his confidence and generosity of spirit. Maybe it was because of his youth or simply because he believed God but, whatever the possible failure of the whole situation, it seemed to have little or no hold on his expectation. I wonder how many people he checked with first before he tapped Jesus' disciples on the shoulder and handed over his lunch. I wonder how many patronizing smiles he received. I love his spirit as he chose to keep moving forward beyond the threat of failure.

When it comes to living a life that steps out in faith rather than shrinks back, I think John the Baptist would be the one who would have to take home the gold medal. There is little to no romance in the way he dressed or looked. He was ruled not by the opinions of others but by the mission he was on. Just picture it: his beard full of locust dribble and his motley animal-skin robe sticky from honey as he cried out to all within earshot: "Repent, repent for the Kingdom of God is at hand". His inner world led his outer world, rather than the other way around. Failure seemed to have little or even no hold on his life.

In the famous parable of the talents, found in Matthew 25:14–30, I believe that the master of these three servants was not as worried about the amount that was produced through the investment of his talents, as he was about his servants having a go. He was not furious about the actual amounts produced by each servant but he was furious over an attitude that said, "I will assume the attitude of failure and thereby attempt nothing". For this master, it was criminal to live cautiously. Failure is not just failing to fulfil our dreams. True failure is allowing past experiences to make us unwilling to take a risk.

The ultimate failure is to no longer be willing to take a risk

---

Here is how the Psalmist described the man who refuses to allow failure to freeze him:

The steps of a good man are ordered by the LORD, And He delights in his way. Though he fall, he shall not be utterly cast down; For the LORD upholds him with His hand. Psalm 37:23–24

Peter, Thomas, the little boy, John the Baptist... nothing confined or reduced their willingness to attempt things for God: no amount of failure; no amount of social ineptness; and no amount of ridicule or thinly disguised tolerance.

For all of us, we have to learn to accept what God says about us, not what failure says about us. We need to be enthusiastic embracers of failure: people who recognize that failure can cause us to move forward, to learn and to grow. We must be prepared to walk a failure pathway, knowing and trusting that it is a pathway towards success. Look at the Psalm again... the steps of a good man, a righteous man, a man whose heart is in tune with the Lord are ordered by Him and He delights in the good man's way. It brings Him joy when we keep moving forward and, even though we fall, and we will, we are not defeated. We can get up again for the Lord upholds us with His hand (Psalm 37:24). That is how we continue into *failure freedom*.

KEY SCRIPTURE

Psalm 37:23–24

REFLECTION

- Are you prepared to keep walking while experiencing a failure pathway?
- What truths do you need to use to confront your fears because of previous failure?
- Are you able, like the baseball batter, to move forward with one victory in three? What attitudes will you need to change?

PRAYER

Lord, You order my steps. Even though I mess up and I don't always understand, today, I am aware of the fact that I need You. Thank you Father that You help me back up when I fall. I will keep my gaze on You and the path that You have directed for me and I will not allow my past to hold me hostage. I choose to sing Your praises as You will never abandon me and I declare You have called me by name.

BE STRONG, BE COURAGEOUS

CHAPTER EIGHT

It is fine to celebrate success, but it is more important to heed the lessons of failure.
Bill Gates

Can I take a moment to once again remind you that God is more committed to what is in front of you than where you have been or even where you are right now? All of us are today setting a foundation for what God wants to do tomorrow.

To have the purposes of God in our future and to live a better tomorrow, we all need to draw on God's help to process the things we have gone through and learn from what hasn't worked, so that we can bring strength to every weakness. We cannot just ignore the areas of failure, forget about them and hope they will go away! If we want to move into failure freedom and gain the most we can from our failures, we must decide actively to face and walk through our failure situations.

What we bring to our failure situation today will actually be reproduced through our lives, in both a positive and a negative sense. Our decision is very important; will we bring fear, risk aversion and avoidance or will we bring faith, courage and strength, and will we learn and move on from past failure?

Our response today sets a foundation for what God can do tomorrow

---

CROSSING YOUR JORDAN

After the death of Moses the servant of the LORD, it came to pass that the LORD spoke to Joshua the son of Nun, Moses' assistant, saying: "Moses My servant is dead. Now therefore, arise, go over this Jordan, you and all this people, to the land which I am giving to them - the children of Israel. Every place that the sole of your foot will tread upon I have given you, as I said to Moses. From the wilderness and this Lebanon as far as the great river, the River Euphrates, all the land of the Hittites, and to the Great Sea toward the going down of the sun, shall be your territory. No man shall be able to stand before you all the days of your life; as I was with Moses, so I will be with you. I will not leave you nor forsake you. Be strong and of good courage, for to this people you shall divide as an inheritance the land which I swore to their fathers to give them. Only be strong and very courageous... "
Joshua 1:1–7

The story of the transition of leadership from Moses to Joshua begins in Deuteronomy and continues into the book of Joshua. I love that Joshua is told to be strong and courageous in three separate occurrences during this transition: firstly, by Moses in Deuteronomy 31:6–7; then by God, Himself, three times (Joshua 1:6–9); and, finally, by the people Joshua is leading, who echo this directive to be strong and courageous (Joshua 1:18).

Joshua is soon going to be faced with a huge challenge, not only in leading this huge nation of people, but in leading them into their

Promised Land. However, there is a massive barrier to cross before even starting to take possession of the land: the Jordan River.

The name 'Jordan' means descending. Do you know that whenever something is on descent, or is failing, as it were, we must be strong and courageous to walk through that? We can't just expect it to change. We can't just ignore it. We need to walk through the failure or challenge. Every Jordan needs to be crossed; every decision or event that has 'descended', or where we have a sense of failure attached, we have to jump into the water and cross that thing.

To face our failures, to learn from them and to purpose to move forward is going to take us doing something. Results require response.

We must make a decision to be strong and courageous even if we don't feel like it. It is under our control to do so. It is so easy to give in to the current-day realities, but I've discovered that we need to wear strength and courage like a badge. It's not about how we feel or what is happening or what is not happening. It's about a decision to bring strength and courage into that situation, in spite of our feelings or what circumstances look like, and to make the changes required.

Winston Churchill said: courage is going from failure to failure without loss of enthusiasm. Bringing strength, courage and enthusiasm to a failure situation doesn't just happen. It takes a pressing in and a commitment to be strong with what God is asking us to do in stepping forward.

What is the Jordan in your life that you need to cross? What is the failure that you need to face? What thoughts or situations do you need to dispossess in order to gain your Promised Land? And who is watching you and learning from how you will respond to the failures and challenges in your life?

A result requires a response

BRING STRENGTH AND COURAGE

To be strong means to fasten upon, to seize, to conquer and continue in. To be courageous is to be alert, be steadfastly minded, fortify, prevail and be obstinate. We are going to need to bring all these qualities as we face our failures head on with strength and courage.

I believe that strength does not come from succeeding all the time but, rather, is formed from our decision not to surrender to our struggle. It is a constant decision to press forward, to keep on going after failure. However, we need to decide that we will be strong and courageous, and that we will keep on going with the mandate that God has given us.

Three months into planting our church, I was preaching one morning and noticed a grey-headed man with a goatee, who came in and sat, with arms crossed and a disapproving look on his face during the whole service. He didn't smile once! He came up to me at the end of the service and said: "Sonny, can I ask you a question? Who are you again?" I said, "Well, I'm Paul de Jong and we just started this church a few months ago." "So what credentials have you got?" he continued on, diminishing my confidence with each attacking question.

I remember standing there feeling smaller and smaller and wanting to run away and hide. I left that building that day more depressed than I've ever been. My thoughts started up, reminding me that, "Yes, actually, I scored only 37% for English. Actually I've always said I could never be a senior pastor." That internal spiral was now fully under way and an echo of doubt almost immediately took centre stage: "I can't do this. This man is right!".

On the drive home with the kids and Maree, I just didn't want to talk. It is hard to describe how flat I felt in that moment and, no matter what I did, I couldn't lift the low-flying cloud that had suddenly engulfed me. We arrived home and, instead of having lunch with my family as usual, I went straight up to my room and cried my eyes out… like a baby. I cried so much I felt like I couldn't cry anymore.

It was at that point, I felt the Holy Spirit fill the room and say, "Paul, who asked you to do this?"

"God, you did," I replied.

"Well then, you've got to understand and embrace the fact that you're the man to do what I've asked you to do."

Right there, I was confronted with what turned out to be a failure-altering revelation. If I wanted to continue to walk forward, doing what God was asking me to do, fulfilling my purpose in Him, I needed to be strong and be courageous. I needed not only to face this situation with strength and courage, but also to see my pathway forward with a sense of faith, strength and courage.

God gave me a moment that day where He reminded me of what I was here to do and why I was doing what I was doing. He reminded me and encouraged me to continue on, even though the circumstances were tough.

In Deuteronomy 31:4, Moses encourages Joshua to remember the God moments: the things God has done in the past and the way He has delivered them.

Doing this builds our strength and courage, as it reminds us of the character of the God we serve. I may not feel strong. I may not feel courageous. But after failure or any disappointment, I must remember that God is with me, that He goes before me and He will never leave me. God was there at the start and He is still there now. It may not look like it and we may not feel like it, but we can decide to be courageous and strong anyway. It is the strength of God's hand that will carry us through our failures to a hope-filled future.

We can believe for so much more when we stop and remember what God has already done

---

KEY SCRIPTURE

Joshua 1:1–7

REFLECTION

- What failure situations in your life seem like Jordans to cross at present?
- How will you determine to build strength and courage in your life?
- Make a list of the things God has done in the past and promised you that will help you stay strong and courageous as you face your failures.

PRAYER

Father, today I need Your whisper in my ear. I need to know from You that I can be strong and courageous. Show me where I am not being strong and have fallen into a pattern of accepting my current limitations. Restore to me a renewed hope that will refuel my strength and courage so I can cross every river in front of me.

FAILURE'S FUEL

PART THREE

FAILURE, OUR EDUCATOR

CHAPTER NINE

A failure is a man who has blundered, but is not capable of cashing in on the experience.
Elbert Hubbard

When a child first begins to colour in, they don't stay within the lines. When they first begin to play catch in the backyard, not every ball is caught. Some are missed and even sent smashing through windows (I certainly was guilty of this on more than one occasion). When a child learns to ride a bike, they will wobble and fall.

What is our usual response as parents? We tell our child not to worry and to have another go. Even if the child is screaming with hurt or wearing the look of great disappointment, we encourage them with, "You'll do better next time".

Never forget that God is the same. His gentle voice comes to us when we go outside the lines, break windows or fall down. He says, "Why do you want to get it right the first time? Don't you realize that your failures are going to educate you?"

Every time you fail, as long as you keep on trying and learn from the past mistake, you will move forward with greater knowledge and wisdom.

As the quote by Elbert Hubbard at the opening of the chapter illustrates, failure is not necessarily trying something and making a mistake but, ultimately, failure is a dominating power only when we fail to learn from that mistake. Failure can actually be great fuel in achieving our dreams, if we allow it to become an educator.

When we stop reacting to failure, we can start learning

The wonder of the message of Christ is that not only does He break the power of failure off us but, if we allow it, He brings our failure to a place where it can become a platform to a greater level of success than we had, even before the failure!

William Singleton wrote:

When it comes to failure, too many people when they make a mistake just keep stubbornly ploughing ahead and end up repeating the same mistakes. I believe in the motto 'try, then stop and think, and try again'.

Not just try and tray again. If you want to be stuck in a repetitive, never-ending cycle of failure, then don't learn from your mistakes. Keep on doing the same thing over and over again, without being willing enough or humble enough to learn, change and grow from your failures. Those of us who do want to change, grow and move forward, however, must follow Singleton's example to try, fail, learn, try better, fail better, learn more... and continue to keep trying beyond our failures. I am so committed to this idea of learning from failure that, if I were to write a dictionary, I would actually define failure as:

Valuable lessons embraced by champions!

One of the most successful companies in our modern era must be Coca-Cola. I'm not saying that the drink is necessarily all that good for us but the company has been incredibly successful. Do you know that, in its first year of operation, it sold only 400 Coke units? That works out to be around seven or eight bottles of Coca-Cola each week. You don't have to be a business person to know that expenses outweighed income that year. I guarantee that, in those early years, the learning curve was immense.

Consider Henry Ford, the founder of the Ford Motor Company. He went through two bankruptcies before he established the Ford Motor Company.

Abraham Lincoln lost seven elections before he finally became president. He didn't see the loss of election after election as a reason to give up but, rather, as something to embrace and learn from.

Each one of these examples illustrates the value of seeing failure as a stepping-stone to something greater. For these people, somehow they were able to weaken the echoes of failure. Their previous failures were able to be fenced and learnt from. Failure became a normal part of the deal; failure did not shut down the show. In fact, in each of these examples, initial failure ultimately led to greatness.

Science is built on this principle. A scientist knows that an experience is never truly a failure. It is always a lesson. Not only that but, in failing, scientists usually learn more than they do from success!

FAILURE AND WISDOM

As believers, we know that wisdom is to be something we seek and develop in our lives. If I were handed two gift boxes – one filled with ongoing prosperity, with no lack of finance or financial need for my whole life, and one filled with wisdom – which would I choose? Assuming we know the Bible, we would choose wisdom. We know it is the right answer. But do we know why? It is because the release of wisdom covers all of life, including the ability to create financial provision.

How do we find wisdom? I believe that failure is a crucial key to finding the wisdom that we seek. Where we may have thought that wisdom was demonstrated in our lives through the absence of failure, I have taken an opposite position. Failure creates stepping-stones into the walk of wisdom. Knowing how to live with failure gives us an amazing advantage.

Wisdom is the result of using failure as a stepping-stone

I speak to leaders all over the world. They don't know what my school report cards said about me. Unless I choose to tell them, they don't know about my many failures at school. My academic achievements at school were few and far between. But I have been a student of life and a student of failure.

Those early failures in tests and other school-based learning caused a lot of trouble. I heard rebukes from teachers and those older than me many times. I had no choice but to learn from my failure to learn: to understand from my failure to understand. I mentioned earlier that for my last year of school, I averaged 37% in English for the entire year. How could someone with that level of academic failure be writing and speaking sermons all over the world, and even have published books (easy-to-read ones!)? It happened because I didn't let that initial failure stop me from moving forward. Although I may not have a natural talent for English, I have been able to learn enough to become a communicator of both the spoken and written word to many thousands of people around the world. To do that, I needed to embrace failure from the right perspective and use my failures to gain valuable learning and wisdom. I needed to, in fact, use my failure as a stepping-stone and motivator to walk into the calling God had on my life. It took effort and it took determination. I needed to shut down the echoes and voices of the past, fence them and ask for help. But by God's grace, I have used failure as a great educator in this area.

My failures are now taking up a shorter amount of my life and they are a better quality of failure. What do I mean when I talk about differing qualities of failure? It is simply that my failures are now stepping-stones towards success and learning platforms towards greater wisdom. We must not keep repeating yesterday's mistakes in yesterday's way. We must fail at a higher level and gain the wisdom we are meant to learn from that failure.

Repeating the same failure is where failure wins

GOD'S DISCIPLINE

My son, do not despise the LORD's discipline, and do not resent his rebuke, because the LORD disciplines those he loves, as a father the son he delights in. Blessed are those who find wisdom, those who gain understanding, for she is more profitable than silver and yields better returns than gold. Proverbs 3:11–14 NIV

When we fail in respect to God, He disciplines us. This proverb explains that not only is that discipline covered in love, but also that it leads us to wisdom. When we add God's love and wisdom into the equation, it looks something like this: we fail; He loves; He disciplines; we grow in wisdom; and we try again, using what we have learned as a platform towards success. Since it is God who is teaching us, we are never diminished or lessened by the rebuke. In fact, here is the amazing truth – embedded in each rebuke is the seed of wisdom.

I don't know about you but I want to be in that school for my whole life – the one where God educates and leads me.

When we come to the end of ourselves because of failure, when there is nothing left to turn to, it is amazing what we find. When we no longer allow failure to dominate us or to have the final say in our lives, we step into extraordinary freedom.

When failure is embraced, we step into extraordinary freedom

When we take the stand that we are only ever going to be a failure, we fail to see that we are standing right on top of possibilities. Sure, there will be some hard work involved but the truth is that we have more inside of us than we realize.

It is a sad thing to see people who have lived such narrow lives because they never embraced the ability to free themselves from failure. With every failure comes a new level of wisdom: the wisdom that comes with learning. Can you see how failures can actually position us for advantage?

KEY SCRIPTURE

Proverbs 3:11–14

REFLECTION

- Can you think of situations where you have 'cashed in' on your failures? How were you able to do that?
- How do you need to commit to failing 'better' in the future?
- Think of times God has brought wisdom to a failure and helped you move forwards. How did you respond to God's gentle discipline or leading?

PRAYER

Lord, I seek Your wisdom for my life and for my past, present and future failures. Lord, I want You to help me value wisdom as You do. Father, give me a heart that is so inclined towards You, that I can truly ask without regret or without pretense as Solomon did, for wisdom is above any other thing.

FAILURE, OUR LAUNCH PAD

CHAPTER TEN

Never confuse a single defeat with a final defeat.
F. Scott Fitzgerald

When we free ourselves to see failure as a good thing, there seems to be an automatic rise of faith in our hearts.

It is when we allow our challenges to become so huge in our minds that we can't find the answers, when we believe things are absolutely out of control, when failure has been given permission to breed and has caused confusion about where to turn next, it is then that we are faced with a decision point, an opportunity to step into a faith dimension as never before.

Faith is more about relationship with a God who is able than it is about a result. Our faith should not, in the first instance, be married to a result: it should be married to the Author of our faith. In the face of our failures, we can be introduced to the God that loves and cares, to the God of all grace and mercy, to the One who can take our brokenness and begin to construct something of value and worth. Yes, there will, most likely, be a change in our circumstances as a result;

but, first and foremost, turning failure into faith will break us into a new level of our relationship with God.

A.R. Fawcett said:

The Lord has more need of our weakness than our strength. Our strength is God's rival. Our weakness is God's servant, drawing on His resources and showing forth His glory. Man's extremity is God's opportunity, whereas man's security is Satan's opportunity. When you think you're strong, you're weak. When you're weak, He's strong.

Turning failure into faith releases new levels of relationship with God

---

LAUNCHED INTO THE FUTURE

We have now learned that failure in itself is not wrong but becomes limiting when it is not dealt with correctly. Failure is a part of life and will ultimately have a good outcome, if we understand its healthy power. I believe that God wants us to use our failures as launch pads into our future.

In the introduction, I suggested that you allow the Holy Spirit to bring up from your memory bank areas of life where you feel you have failed. I hope you are doing that. It is a powerful tool.

Is it possible now for you to see every one of those occasions as an amazing launch pad into an area of life and influence that you would not have had otherwise? That is how this faith of ours works. Remember Joseph? When he finally stood in front of his brothers, as they bowed before him – the fulfilment of those early dreams – he said these words recorded in Genesis 50:20

But as for you, you meant evil against me; but God meant it for good, in order to bring it about as it is this day, to save many people alive.

Whether we have brought failure on ourselves, or others have failed us, every single thing that has happened in our lives can become a launch pad to a future of influence and greater freedom!

God is fully embedded in every part of our journey

In recent years, much has been preached and written about Jabez, an obscure Old Testament character. In 1 Chronicles 4:10, Jabez prayed:

"Oh, that you would bless me indeed, and enlarge my territory, that Your hand would be with me, and that You would keep me from evil, that I may not cause pain!"

Jabez was born in pain. His name actually means pain. However, he came to a point where he drew a boundary around the circumstances of his early life. He called on the God of Israel and prayed this most impacting prayer.

Here is the question: Would he have prayed that prayer if everything in his life had been perfect? No, he would not have needed to. Life had not been perfect for Jabez and he used his flawed past to launch himself into a vision-filled request to the Lord. And the Bible says God granted him what he requested.

It is important to note the direction into which he launched himself. He could have so easily done what so many do today. He could have let the past launch him into bitterness, cynicism, rebellion or deceit. Today, the failures of life launch too many towards these things, in addition to drugs, and/or destructive relationships, and/or self-harm and/or criticism. Not so with Jabez. He chose the trajectory for his launch. It was going to be nowhere else but towards the purposes and plans that God had for him.

Jabez chose the trajectory of his future; choose yours

We need to do the same. We need to determine that: failure will not launch us in a trajectory of risk aversion, fear or condemnation; that it will not decrease our faith but, rather, increase it; and that it will not drive us away from God but directly into His arms, even more so than it does when things are going well.

What does the Bible say about how God can restore after failure? In the book of Joel, the prophet Joel is speaking to Judah about their past failures and the coming judgment because of their turning away from God. However, read what God promises to do, if they repent, turn towards Him and start living right:

I will repay you for the years the locusts have eaten - the great locust and the young locust, the other locusts and the locust swarm - my great army that I sent among you. You will have plenty to eat, until you are full, and you will praise the name of the LORD your God, who has worked wonders for you; never again will my people be shamed. Then you will know that I am in Israel, that I am the LORD your God, and that there is no other; never again will my people be shamed. Joel 2:25–28 NIV

Hannah, another Old Testament hero, gives us an amazing picture into this idea of failure providing us with a launch pad into a great future. Her failure, according to the understanding of the day, was her barren womb. She didn't deserve this. She didn't ask for this. She was just barren – a heartbreaking thing. Like Jabez, she also made sure of the direction her launch pad faced. She faced it to God, not away from Him. In effect, she said, "I'm not going to allow what seems to be right, to be right. You're the God that says children are our heritage. Even though You shut up my womb, I am going to stand here and I'm going to present my failure in a position of faith."

Once we decide that our failure will bow its knee to faith, we unlock the supernatural

God responded. The great prophet Samuel was born.

We can look at our failure and think, "That's it!" but God says, "No! I am looking for somebody, somewhere, who will lift beyond their failure and place a reach, a demand, on heaven that will attract supernatural power, and who will allow their failure to bring light into the world."

God is looking for people who won't allow their current realities to dictate their futures. The nations of the earth need people who look past their natural and current states. What would a generation of people, who draw boundaries around failure, aim their launch pads in the right direction and fire into a faith-filled future, look like? I know some of those kinds of people. They bring hope into a dismal world!

Victory is a person who won't allow their current realities to be the final outcome

To direct our launch pad towards God after failure, instead of towards bitterness, cynicism, frozenness or a myriad of other responses, we must determine to arise in faith. We must not be so concerned about the source of our 'failure' as in: "Did God orchestrate this, as He did with Hannah? Is this Satan? Did I bring this on myself? Am I a victim?" Instead, we need to use the tools mentioned earlier, use fences, ask for accountability and embrace our failure. Then we need to place ourselves into a realm of faith to receive God's next move. God will always have a step forward out of any failure and it is up to us to seek Him until we hear what that next move is.

KEY SCRIPTURE

1 Chronicles 4:10

REFLECTION

- What does failure tend to launch you towards? Is it bitterness, cynicism or risk aversion? Or is it faith and new learning?
- How have your failures brought you to a new level in your relationship with God and your faith?
- List people you could influence and lead through what you have learnt from your past failures.

PRAYER

Father, today, I make a decision to look beyond my circumstances, beyond my current difficulties and forward into a life of hope, faith and promise: a life that You have waiting for me and have written for me before my first breath. Lord, I will use where I am today as a starting point, a launch pad, for where I want to be and I commit this to You in faith. Thank you in advance, Father. Thank you that Your promises to me are 'Yes' and 'Amen'!

CULTIVATING THE CRY

CHAPTER ELEVEN

Our greatest glory is not in never failing, but in rising up every time we fail.
Ralph Waldo Emerson

Scripture is full of challenges, such as in Luke 18:8b: *"... when the Son of Man comes, will He really find faith on the earth?"*

I believe Jesus is going to come back to some of the slickest churches you've ever seen. We are doing church better now than we've ever done it before – great lights, great worship, great environments and happy people. But Jesus says (I am paraphrasing), "I have a problem. When I come back, I don't know how much faith I will find. I think there will be a whole lot of hope, which is the beginning of faith, but I don't know how much raw faith there will be."

Before Jesus spoke of His concerns about levels of faith, He had already told this parable in Luke 18 to His disciples (I am paraphrasing):

There was a widow woman in the city. She had nothing except enough courage and desperation to go for help. She chose to go to the town judge to tell him of her need and to see what he could do for her. Sadly, the town judge was without mercy and without basic humanity. He didn't care for mankind and he had no belief in any higher power. He was a daunting prospect. But this widow's needs were so great that she refused to take his first dismissal as the final story for her life. She went back to him... again... and again. In effect, she was saying, "I'm at a place of failure and, by coming to you, I am positioning myself for a better life".

He dug his heels in and virtually said, "Because you are annoying me, I am less and less likely to help". She responded, "If you don't help me, know that I'll just stand at the front gate and, when you go home tonight, I'll be following you. Then, when you go into your house and shut your door, I'm going to use my loud voice to walk up and down your street saying, 'Judge, you will help me!'" She wore him down and he met her need.

Jesus finished His story. Perhaps He waited a while until it sunk in, this story of radical and ridiculous faith. Then He drove the parable home with an outrageous declaration: (Again, I am paraphrasing) Your father in heaven works in the same way. Just when we think God is not interested and does not care whether justice is done in our lives, we hear this parable and find that He is listening and watching intently.

Here is what we have to learn.

Firstly, we have to cultivate a cry for help.

This cry must go beyond singing songs in a service. It is the cry that is on our lips as we wake up in the morning. It is the cry that says, "God, I can lean on you and I can draw from you".

The intensity of our cry reflects the desperation of our heart

---

Years ago, when I was a youth pastor, I remember a young punk rocker came to our youth group on the invitation of a school friend.

She came up to me at the end of the message with an unrelenting stare and said what is said so often: "The problem with you Christians is that you all need a crutch". I didn't have a great answer at that time but I wish we could meet again now because I have the answer. I would say: "You're right. I was born with a need for a crutch. In fact, we all were. My crutch is the need of a God who understands, brings strength from my weakness and wants to walk with me as Saviour and friend for the rest of my life. Oh, and by the way, we all have a crutch and for some of us it is the need to look like our friends."

Oh, if we would realize that our needs and failures can position us for an amazing life of faith.

The greater our need, the greater the level of God's corresponding strength

---

As we cultivate our cry for help, we shift ourselves from being passive and fatalistic to being noisy and insistent. As a father of boys, I knew about noisy and insistent. To get their attention, I didn't waste my time with a quiet, "Okay, teenagers". No, I had to get through to them. It was more like: "GUYS!" When we cultivate this cry, it is not to gain God's attention as I did with my sons. No, God hears our faintest cry. Rather, it is for us to hear our own cry; to clarify what is in our hearts.

This parable in Luke 18 has a powerful message: in our failure, in this time of pressure, in our current position – economic relational and/or spiritual – we need to cultivate the cry of faith.

Failure weakens the moment we let God in

There is a real-life example of this tucked neatly and famously into the Old Testament. It is the story of another kind of cultivated cry. A godly man, Mordecai, carefully and cleverly positioned his niece,

Esther, as the new queen of the godless King Ahasuerus. In a time of threatened genocide, Mordecai told Esther to go before the King and demand help for her people. She reminded her uncle that a sure death awaited her but then bravely said, "If I perish, I perish".

Then her cultivated cry took on a very clever sound – a look, in fact. Her people and her staff fasted for three days and then she put on her very best clothes. She already smelt beautiful. Her bathing routine had been well established for some time – oils and perfumes had made her a most appealing woman. She stood outside the King's door and it wasn't long before his nostrils twitched. He was surrounded by soldiers and the room smelt like a mosh pit at a rock 'n' roll concert. Esther's perfume was something else and he liked it… a lot. What I love about this story is that she not only included others in her cultivated cry, but she prepared and committed to it with 100% commitment. A knock opened the door but the cultivated cry had already opened the King's heart.

If our voice is not desperate, will we see the wonder of what God can do?

Desperation is the tone that activates a heavenly response

When our youngest son Daniel was around nine or 10 years of age, he loved animals – dogs, cats, frogs, mice – basically anything with four legs.

I will never forget Daniel giving me a long cuddle, one time when I was about to fly out to speak internationally. He sat on my knee and said, "Dad, can I pray for you before you go?" I was surprised and moved by his request.

He put his hand on my head and began, "Father, we pray that you bless Daddy. Help him to preach good." He even shook his hand on my head a little, as he had seen a preacher do somewhere.

When he finished, I was a mess; he had so touched my heart. Then he said, "Dad, have you thought any more about the axolotls?"

I replied, "Mate, I don't even know what they are." He reminded me that we had already talked about them. I told him that I had forgotten that conversation. So, he obliged and continued, "They are the Mexican walking fish. You get them and you put them in the fish tank and – you've got to get this, Dad – you feed them real meat."

By now, I was totally in the conversation. I made 'wow' noises.

He continued, "When we go away on holidays, you can leave goldfish in the tank and they'll attack the goldfish."

By now, my very melted heart had a reality check. I had been on a high with his earnest and unexpected prayer of blessing. Now, I realized that his motivation was to get some axolotls!

I think he even texted me on Maree's phone when I was overseas: "axolotl?"

When I arrived home, the first thing he said to me was, "Did you think about the axolotl?"

A couple of months later, I opened my Bible and out falls a piece of paper with "axolotls?" written in his handwriting.

Yes, I am sure you know where this is going… we ended up buying him two Mexican walking fish! Is that bad parenting? I'm not sure, but it was our response to a persistent and cultivated cry.

MOTIVE ALIGNMENT

Once we embrace failure and allow it to activate new levels of faith, we are already living in a new and wonderful place in God. But, in learning to cultivate a cry after failure, we must address the matter of aligning our motives with the heart of God. You see, it is not just a matter of crying over every desire and drifting into a 'game' mentality with God. It is vital that we take time to examine our heart after failure, because, if our heart is right, our asking is right.

It is true that it is easy to become confused about what is and isn't God's will, especially after we have stepped out and failed. The way I view the answer to this now, though, is quite simple. We must answer the question: "Is my heart in a position that I would really do whatever God wanted me to do?" As challenging as that question is, when we lay down self and are prepared to do whatever God wants us to do, we begin to see faith kick in over our failure.

When self is positioned second, God is free to take charge

It is all to do with our motives.

Let me give you an example. I moved from New Zealand to Sydney in 1981. I knew that the move to Australia was in God but, now that I was living in Sydney, the opportunity came to move north to subtropical Brisbane. For five months, I asked God to tell me what He wanted me to do. The heavens were like brass. As far as I could tell, I was not predisposed to one option over another but I do remember praying, "God, what if I stay in Sydney and my wife is in Brisbane? I don't want to just do what seems to be the best. I want to do what You want. I know You called me to Australia but I don't know what to do now."

After five months, this is what God said to me, "What do you want to do?" It came very clearly to me. I replied, "I want to do what You want me to do." He returned with, "Then I want to do what you want to do."

When our hearts are aligned with His heart, we want what He wants and there are times when He wants what we want. Our motive is everything.

Rather than being paralysed by indecision and not knowing what the will of God is, when we live with our hearts soft and yielded to the Lord, God takes care of moving our hearts, and then the rest of us, into the right place. We become free from procrastination and we move forward.

After being married to Maree for many years, the truth is that the closer we become to each other, the more we can speak freely to each other and the more we can ask of each other. In the church we lead in Auckland, the team works out of relationship. We aren't doing jobs, we are doing life together. I can ask things of this team because we work in an environment of relationship.

James takes us to the place of motive-checking with this powerful statement:

But if you have bitter envy and self seeking in your hearts, do not boast and lie against the truth. This wisdom does not descend from above, but is earthly, sensual, demonic. For where envy and self-seeking exist, confusion and every evil thing are there. But the wisdom that is from above is first pure; then peaceable, gentle, willing to yield, full of mercy and good fruits, without partiality and without hypocrisy. Now the fruit of righteousness is sown in peace by those who make peace. James 3:14–18

When our hearts are filled with self, our motives are going to be shaky at best and evil at worst. No wonder we end up confused. But, when our hearts are aligned to the things of God, heaven is stirred and the cultivated cry of bold faith is met.

The great pattern of prayer that is found in Luke 11 starts with: Our Father in heaven, Hallowed be Your name. When we are cultivating our cry to God, we start by recognizing who our heavenly Father is. Even though we come to Him with the persistency that moves the heart of a heartless judge, we know that He is not heartless and that He does indeed care! How important it is that we bring our failures to Him, crying out with persistence for His wisdom, His next step and His breakthrough for our situation. The second line of the prayer addresses our heart motive: Your Kingdom come, Your will be done...

– encouraging us to keep asking in line with God's will and heart. Once we have these elements, we are able to cultivate a cry to see heaven move earth.

We ask and keep on asking. Can I encourage you to cultivate the cry of 'the ask' in your failures. Bring them to God, ask and keep on asking, until you see failure freedom come into all areas of your life.

KEY SCRIPTURE

Luke 18:1–8

REFLECTION

- At the beginning of this chapter, we read from Luke 18:8b: "… when the Son of Man comes, will He really find faith on the earth?" What would your answer be if that question were asked of your own life?
- Can you think of an example of where you have cultivated a cry of faith to God: where you have asked and asked again, and been persistent for a breakthrough?
- What area(s) of failure and lack do you need to cultivate a committed cry in?

PRAYER

Father, I know that I need to learn this lesson of being persistent in prayer and cultivating a cry, even when I want to give up. Lord, remind me of the parable of the persistent widow so that the next time I don't see results and get impatient, I will press on in prayer, knowing that Your timing is perfect and that You are a good God and that You answer my prayers when I ask with the right motives.

FOCUSING THE DREAM

CHAPTER TWELVE

Failures are finger posts on the road to achievement
C.S Lewis

Having moved from the hopelessness of failure to a new level of certainty and trust in God's ability to bring us into places of faith and victory, there is now one more thing to do.

We need to focus the dream. What is it that we carry in our heart with a passion? That special something that God has given to each of us. Even when we feel lost in failure, God has a dream for our lives that He has held since before we were formed.

If God has a plan for us, we have a future

The prophet Jeremiah described it like this: *"For I know the plans I have for you," declares the LORD, "plans to prosper you and not to harm you, plans to give you hope and a future"* Jeremiah 29:11 NIV.

We can lose that dream or never find it in the first place, when we are caught up in failure. However, as we continue to move through failure freeze to failure freedom, we must make further conscious effort to focus the dream. It is possible to lose the dream that we have been given from God after failure. We want to give up, we start to question and, of course, the enemy's plan is to stop us from even dreaming. However, after failure is the most important time to focus on our dream, hone the details and reiterate what we are here for and what God is asking us to do.

When we arrived in Auckland in 1991, we had a dream to build a great church for God, but the dream went way beyond that. Deep down we wanted to do something that would ultimately change our city, influence our nation and touch our world. By God's grace, we are seeing that dream coming to pass. It would be so easy to say that, because God called us and He has been with us, it has been easy. But, far from it! There have been many times throughout the different seasons when I have felt that I was in way over my head. I have discovered that, if we are trying to get it right, then God will walk with us; and, at the times where mistakes are made, as long as we keep walking, learning and committing to do our best, God will use everything.

Perseverance is such a powerful tool to have in our life, if the dream we carry is going to have an opportunity to take root and grow. For me at least, it has been a commitment to focus on the dream and not on the disappointments that will be a part of every one of our journeys.

When we focus on the finish line, we release the energy needed to get there. Just like you, I have needed to make a determined decision so many times to put deliberate energy into shifting my focus from failures back to the dream.

When we focus on the finish line, we release the energy needed to get there

---

I love this scripture in James 1, in The Message. It talks about how difficulties, including failures, can actually be seen as gifts. They can actually hone, mature and develop our dreams:

Consider it a sheer gift, friends, when tests and challenges come at you from all sides. You know that under pressure, your faith-life is forced into the open and shows its true colors. So don't try to get out of anything prematurely. Let it do its work so you become mature and well-developed, not deficient in any way. James 1:1–3 MSG

When I look back at the failures I have had in living out the dream that God has given me, they have actually been gifts. I have matured and developed in a way I never would have done without those challenges. I have focused on my dreams more as an outcome of failure. Failures have made me more determined, not less, to see through what God has asked me to do. What about you? Can you use your failures to focus your dream again?

What we focus on determines where we end up

FAILURE'S FRUIT

New Zealand suffered an immense school tragedy in 2008. There was a class of students from a Christian school who were on a leadership-development trip and, due to circumstances beyond the control of the school, one of the teachers and six students drowned in a freak, weather-related canyoning accident.

Our church, along with many others, did all we could to support the school and some of the families in dealing with such a horrific situation.

After this, the parents and sister of one of the boys who had lost their lives came to our church to thank us. Their son and brother was an incredible musician and so many testified that he was totally committed to God and had introduced them to Jesus.

As we talked with his family that morning, they shared how they were facing the challenge of such a huge loss and how they needed to take it one day at a time. I remember them saying in such open honesty: "It is hard to lose somebody that is so much a part of our life. Every day, we have God. He gives us manna (the supply needed) and strength for each day."

There were no easy answers and no one was pretending. In fact, one of our sons was on that trip and a number that died were his very close classmates. Still, today, there is much residual pain and the sense of loss is deep. Maree and I will never forget the darkness that surrounded our son; it was almost as though we lost him for a year and a half, as he had to find God for himself in the darkness of despair and disappointment. I can't even begin to imagine the depth of pain each of the many families had to carry in the loss of a son or daughter.

I remember in a quiet time saying to God: "I don't get it. I know You are sovereign but it just is so unfair that most were so young and the pain is so deep." I remember saying to our son that if he could find God in this darkness, he would discover a depth and understanding of God that many Christians may never experience. I realized that this was a journey I couldn't walk out for him. He had our full support but only God could bring him through it.

While praying during this time, God took me to John 15, where we read that the Father is the owner of the vineyard and Jesus is the vine-dresser. God ultimately wants to produce great fruit that has eternal value from the branches.

In the horrendous loss and darkness of the unexplainable, there was a promise that, even in this tragedy, eternal fruit was guaranteed to come to pass, even though at great cost. These young people, whose earthly lives were over, had influenced so many of their own peers in the preceding years because of their faith and full commitment to God.

I had an opportunity to share some of these things with this family and the mother began to cry. She said, "That is what my husband has just been saying to me."

I believe our real reason for existence is not in the pr ority of a prosperous life here on earth, even though God is committed to blessing us. Our real reason for existence is beyond discovering a great marriage partner, even though, again, God is committed to building amazing marriages. Rather, I believe we are here to discover who God is personally and to be in relationship with Him, while helping others discover His love, forgiveness and purpose. We are here to achieve the purpose He has for our lives and to be ready to be able to bring Him worship for eternity!

Maybe you have gone through some devastating and deeply wounding things in life and today you feel that your future is completely over. Can I encourage you that, no matter what life dishes up, no matter how often we have failed or others have failed us, God has a future for us, if we don't allow failure the right of taking centre stage.

Either failure or future takes centre stage

With God's help, we can turn our "Why, God?" into, "What for, God?" The enemy's plan will not continue and the potential of all that God has for us will be released.

A God future requires that we turn our 'why' into 'what for'

Our great victory over Satan's destroying nature is to embrace our failures and use them to take us forwards, not backwards. We need to use them to focus our dream more strongly than we have ever done before and to achieve even more than we would have, had we never failed!

Satan's DNA is to steal, kill and destroy. He will continue to take from us what God has given us. He wants to shut us down and there is nothing as effective as failure to do that.

But we won't! We will spend eternity bringing uninhibited worship to the King of all kings and it will be then and only then that we will understand clearly the 'why'. Paul writes in 1 Corinthians 13 that, here on earth, we will never fully understand the 'why'.

For now we see in a mirror, dimly, but then face to face. Now I know in part, but then I shall know just as I also am known. And now abide faith, hope, love, these three; but the greatest of these is love. 1 Corinthians 13:12–13

Can you see how we must not allow the things of this age – the failures and even the so-called successes – to throw us off track?

I am not for a moment comparing this terrible school tragedy to failure; however, the lessons can be the same. Just as we and our son and all those affected by this tragedy needed to determine that it would not take us out of the game, we also needed to make a choice. The toughest things can either push us further away from God or pull us closer to Him. We must not allow failure to smother itself like an unending blanket over our hopes,

---

If we allow failure to breathe, it will continue to spread until it dominates

---

energy, dreams and possibilities. Instead, when we fail or are confronted with failure, we must commit to holding onto our dreams, rather than laying them down. Failure is a part of the pasts of all of us and will be a part of our future too, but, if we commit to learn what we need to from the failure, repent when we fail God and change as we need to, we will, ultimately, move beyond the limitations of what happened yesterday and set a God environment where eternal fruit will emerge.

For sure, we can wish certain things hadn't happened but we must hear the voice of our loving God say, "For eternity's sake, put your past sin failures under the blood of My Son, Jesus, and walk away from them. Where you have failed when trying to succeed, don't stop, but learn from those experiences and use them as future stepping-stones. Commit to move forward into all I still have for you."

Thank God that He has a future for you that will build on all the experiences of your past.

KEY SCRIPTURE

Jeremiah 29:11

REFLECTION

- Identify where failure has dulled your dreams or caused you to lower your expectations around it.
- How can you use your failures to cause your dream to have even more focus than it had before?
- Make the commitment to let go of your past and resurrect your dream today. Commit to failure freedom.

PRAYER

Father, thank you for having plans to prosper me and not to harm me. Thank you that You have always believed in me and given me a hope and future. Thank you for resurrecting dreams. Thank you that I don't have to live with the echo of past failures but that I can move forward with hope and faith. Thank you for loving me today and that my best days are ahead. Thank you.

CLOSING THOUGHTS

I have been able to write this book only because I have walked the journey of failure freedom myself: from living so much of my early life being frozen by failure to a place today where failure has become a platform of learning and growth. I know what it is like to fail and to experience the dryness that comes into the human heart when we do. I also know the strength that comes from being able to truly see failure through the lens of faith.

Faith does not necessarily promise an immediate result but it immediately promises a return

As we come to the end of this book, let me encourage you that, if you are serious about gaining freedom in your life, you won't find full satisfaction and success without a personal relationship with Jesus. He desires to be your source of healing, forgiveness and strength. If you have never invited Him to become the centre of your world, or you once did but your relationship is not strong now, I encourage you to take that step and ask Jesus to become your Lord, Saviour and best friend.

In the introduction, I encouraged you to take note of: those things in your life which you saw as failures; the things that made you cringe and want to hide; and the things that had frozen you. I asked you to identify where you were sitting in the grandstand and the areas in which you were living with a risk-averse mentality.

I truly believe that, as you walk forward, reading and applying the principles we have talked about, truth will settle in your heart and mind, and you, too, will live in *failure freedom* in all areas.

As you commit to shutting down the echoes, fencing in the thoughts and actions of the past, embracing accountability and walking away from the grandstands of inactivity, you will start a journey of great faith and freedom. As you determine to embrace your failures as learning opportunities and let them launch you into a place of faith, you will be free to live out the plan God has for you. That plan will impact not only you for eternity, but so many others in your world, as you commit to walking in the freedom that God offers.

And He said to me, "*My grace is sufficient for you, for My strength is made perfect in weakness.*" 2 Corinthians 12:9